ELITE • 202

The British Army since 2000

JIM TANNER

ILLUSTRATED BY PETER DENNIS

Series editor Martin Windrow

First published in Great Britain in 2014 by Osprey Publishing
PO Box 883, Oxford, OX1 9PL, UK
PO Box 3985, New York, NY 10185-3985, USA
E-mail: info@ospreypublishing.com

Osprey Publishing is part of the Osprey Group

A CIP catalogue record for this book is available from the British Library

Print ISBN: 978 1 78200 593 3
PDF ebook ISBN: 978 1 78200 594 0
ePub ebook ISBN: 978 1 78200 595 7

Editor: Martin Windrow
Index by Zoe Ross
Typeset in Sabon and Myriad Pro
Originated by PDQ Media, Bungay, UK
Printed in China through Worldprint Ltd

14 15 16 17 18   10 9 8 7 6 5 4 3 2 1

Osprey Publishing is supporting the Woodland Trust, the UK's leading woodland conservation charity, by funding the dedication of trees.

www.ospreypublishing.com

BACK COVER, LOWER PHOTO L/Cpl Armstrong and Pte Robertson of 3rd Bn Mercian Regt demonstrate typical infantry kit during 'Herrick XIV' in 2011, when their battalion was part of 3rd Commando Brigade. Note the 66mm Light Anti-Structure Missile, and LUCIE binocular night-vision sight. (RHQ Mercian)

ACKNOWLEDGEMENTS

Without the assistance of a large number of individuals this book would have been impossible, and I am indebted to them all for their help. The British Army has a complicated structure, made more so by changes currently under way. These details, and the intricacies of the latest combat clothing and personal equipment, were challenges that could only be overcome by calling on those with current experience. They all had far better things to do than answer my lists of questions, but all gave of their time unfailingly. Special thanks go to: Army HQ – Col Simon Banton, Col Patrick Crowley, Mr Richard Watt; Light Dragoons – Lt Col Sam Plant, Maj John Godfrey, Capt Andrew Werner, 2Lt Ed Holford-Walker; Princess of Wales's Royal Regiment – Col (Retd) Wayne Harber, Maj (Retd) Stephen Bream, Maj (Retd) Giles Clapp, Capt Dave Thomas, Capt Oliver Keith; Royal Fusiliers – Brig (Retd) Ian Liles; Mercian Regiment – LtCol (Retd) Richard Spiby, Maj Andy Ryan, Capt Pete Shergold, Capt Austin Miller, WO2 Greg Hedges; Staffordshire Regiment Museum – Maj (Retd) Jim Massey, Mrs Dani Pritchard; Parachute Regiment – LtCol Mike Shervington, Maj (Retd) Paul Rodgers, Capt John Martin, Pte Tom Courtney; RLC – Maj Russ Hillis, WO1 (Conductor) Bob Graham; MoD – Mr Neil Hall; Imperial War Museum – Mr Ian Proctor, Mr Alan Wakefield; CQC Ltd – Charlotte Davie. Finally, to my colleagues at DB for providing writing time in Riyadh and, especially, to Richard Marshall for his expertise with graphics. Any errors are, of course, entirely those of the author.

All picture credits are shown in the captions to photographs.

I hope this book does justice to Thomas (and now Thomasina) Atkins, that unfailingly cheerful and natural soldier. Half of the fee received by the author will go to the Army Benevolent Fund – the Soldiers' Charity.

ARTIST'S NOTE

Readers may care to note that the original paintings from which the colour plates in this book were prepared are available for private sale. All reproduction copyright whatsoever is retained by the Publishers. All enquiries should be addressed to:

Peter Dennis, Fieldhead, The Park, Mansfield, Nottinghamshire NG18 2AT, UK

The Publishers regret that they can enter into no correspondence upon this matter.

Abbreviations used in this text, in addition to standard abbreviations of unit designations:	
AI	armoured infantry
ARRC	Allied Rapid Reaction Corps (NATO)
AVLB	Armoured Vehicle Launched Bridge
AVRE	Armoured Vehicle Royal Engineers
BAOR	British Army of the Rhine
CCS	combat command support
CDS	Chief of the Defence Staff
CGS	Chief of the (Army) General Staff
CJO	Chief of Joint Operations
CLF	Commander Land Forces
CS	close support (artillery)
CSS	combat service support
EOD	explosive ordnance disposal
ESS	Eye Safety Systems
FAS 2004	Future Army Structure (review, 2004)
FIS 2004	Future Infantry Structure (review, 2004)
GOC	General Officer Commanding
HQLF	Headquarters Land Forces
ISAF	International Security Assistance Force (Afghanistan)
JRRF	Joint Rapid Reaction Force
LI	light infantry
MoD	Ministry of Defence
MOLLE	Modular Lightweight Load-carrying Equipment
Options	Options for Change (review, 1990)
PLCE	Personal Load-Carrying Equipment
PRR	Personal Role Radio
SDR 1998	Strategic Defence Review (1998)
SDSR 2010	Strategic Defence & Security Review (2010)
SJC	Standing Joint Commander
STA	surveillance and target acquisition
TA	Territorial Army
TRF	Tactical Recognition Flash
UAV	unmanned aerial vehicle ('drone')
UKSF	United Kingdom Special Forces
UOR	Urgent Operational Requirements programme

CONTENTS

THE BRITISH ARMY SINCE 2000

INTRODUCTION

While slightly outside the main timeframe of this book, this iconic picture symbolizes the approaching end of the longest continuous operation ever undertaken by the British Army - Operation 'Banner'. Here, in 1998, Cpl Walker of 1st Bn Staffordshire Regt enters Woodbourne security forces base at the end of the Army's last foot patrol in West Belfast. (Staffords Museum)

The British Army has undergone constant change to meet the many and conflicting challenges of war and peace that it has faced since its acknowledged beginnings some 350 years ago in the 17th century. Expansion, contraction and reorganization have punctuated those centuries in order to meet actual and perceived threats. Attempting to explain the evolution of the names of infantry units over just the past 200 years would require a small book in itself. Take, merely as an example, one of today's new 'large/large regiments' – The Rifles – and trace just one of the antecedent units of its 1st Battalion back to its origins as the 99th (later, Lanarkshire) Regiment of Foot in 1824;

or investigate how The Rifles in 2012 came to include in its five Regular battalions two light infantry, one armoured infantry, one mechanized infantry and one commando battalion. There is no place in a book of this size for more than the briefest glance at such complexities as they have surfaced in the past 25 years.

Osprey last gave the modern British Army detailed coverage in 1987 in Mike Chappell's Elite 14, *The British Army in the 1980s*. That army then contained about 160,000 Regular soldiers and more than 70,000 in the Territorial Army. Soon the Regulars will have reduced to about half their 1987 figure, while the strength of the Territorials will be, on paper at least, around the 30,000 mark. The intervening years have seen major reductions and reorganizations, and new roles and deployments, as a result of the world's ever-changing political realities. The army of 1987, while dealing with the major challenges of the 'Troubles' in Northern Ireland, and

manning a number of overseas garrisons, was also squarely focused on the threat posed by the Warsaw Pact. To face the latter more than one-third of the army was stationed in the British Army of the Rhine, with four fighting divisions allotted to 1st (British) Corps. By 2009 the one remaining division in Germany contained just two brigades, with all remaining troops due to be withdrawn by 2018. Reorganization is one thing; but the Army also had to shift its whole mind-set away from the armoured/nuclear battlefield to the demands of major counter-insurgency operations overseas and, as this book goes to print, to their aftermath.

The purpose of this book, while it cannot hope to be a fully comprehensive account, is to provide a concisely detailed description of the British Army during the first decade and a half of the 21st century. To put the army of today in context, it has been necessary not only to list the main organizational changes since 2000, but also to track the earlier restructuring resulting from the end of the Cold War and the two main defence reviews in 1990 (Options for Change, or 'Options') and 1998 (the Strategic Defence Review, 'SDR'). The last decade of the 20th century also saw the final years of major military efforts in Northern Ireland, and peacekeeping operations in the Balkans and elsewhere. These all shaped the army of 2000.

The army that began the new century had settled down after Options, with new organizations in place for a number of regiments, and major restructuring of the majority of the services. But operational roles were still largely the same, and it looked very much like the army of the previous decade, having in those years adopted new combat uniforms and much new equipment. In mid-decade the Army, while getting to grips with two serious wars in Iraq and Afghanistan, underwent some of its most dramatic changes with, in effect, the final demise

The British Army's pride in faultlessly executed ceremonial traditions is typified by the Welsh Guards trooping their Colour before Her Majesty on Horse Guards Parade, London, in June 2013. This annual ceremony marks the Sovereign's official birthday, and each regiment of Foot Guards takes it in turn, supported by other elements of the Household Division. In the foreground are the King's Troop RHA, and in the background the Household Cavalry Mounted Regiment. These are not mere 'chocolate-box' soldiers, however; foremost they are trained to fight, and any spectator will notice a considerable number of campaign medals and some gallantry decorations on the chests of the Guardsmen marching past.
(Crown Copyright 2013)

Iraq, 2006: a soldier from 1st Bn Staffordshire Regt wearing Desert Disruptive Pattern Material (DPM) combat uniform and armed with a Minimi Light Machine Gun (LMG). This effective weapon, first deployed in large numbers on 'Telic 1' in 2003, has entirely replaced the unpopular SA80 Light Support Weapon (LSW) in front-line service. He wears Kestrel body armour, introduced in late 2005 as interim protection ahead of the introduction of Osprey armour late that year. Note the standard Personal Load-Carrying Equipment (PLCE) worn in preference to Modular Lightweight Load-carrying Equipment (MOLLE) pouches attached to the armour carrier, and the issued goggles. (Staffords Museum)

of the old 'regimental system' established under the Cardwell-Childers reforms of the 1870s. The Future Army Structure (FAS) announced in 2004 necessarily receives close examination in these pages.

New structures, new badges, new uniforms and much new equipment were all in place by the close of that decade. Then the biggest transformation of all was announced, with the Strategic Defence and Security Review (SDSR) of 2010. The resultant 'Army 2020' will be organized very differently from the army that has gone before. Throughout, this story must be told against the backdrop of operations in Iraq and Afghanistan. The overall result is an army that, while thoroughly grounded in its past, looks vastly different from even 15 years ago, but which, for its size, has considerable capability in its units and its brigades.

The Army's equipment has also changed dramatically. The focus on conventional warfare emphasised heavy armour and anti-tank weapons. The major counter-insurgency campaigns overseas, while employing some heavy armour, have seen the introduction, usually by way of 'urgent operational requirements' (UORs), of fleets of heavily protected lighter vehicles. A wide array of additional small arms and support weapons have also been brought into service, and 2004 saw the initial issue of the long-awaited Bowman digital communications system. In 1980 platoon commanders still carried whistles, and needed them; by 2005 every infantryman in the ranks had a Personal Role Radio (PRR). Comprehensive details of all the separate items of uniform and equipment cannot be included in a book of this modest size, but much is shown and identified in the photographs and colour plates.

No attempt is made here to comment on policy decisions. Nor can justice be done to every organization in the Army (including the training organization), or to organizational details at unit level. It should be noted, too, that this text has been written during a period of huge change, with some details pertaining to Army 2020 still fluid at the time of writing.

THE ARMY'S ROLE & CHARACTER

Tasks

The Army's role is traditionally defined within a set of military tasks drawn from the Defence Planning Assumptions. These tasks are reconfirmed or redefined in each security review, and thus most recently in SDSR 2010. These reviews set out the overall contribution of the whole armed forces to national security, from defence of the UK to the projection of military power overseas, and, as a result of SDSR, henceforth they are to take place every five years. While based on an overall plan, the Army's own contribution naturally depends on the requirements of each operation being undertaken as well as any enduring commitments.

Much of this book focuses on an army based on the outcome of SDR 1998, albeit that for much of the intervening period it was also repeatedly reorganized to deal with combat and stabilization operations in Iraq and Afghanistan. The 'Army 2020' study of 2012 concluded that 'strategic circumstances dictate that the Army needs to evolve so that it can face future threats effectively'. In essence, the Army would move on from its current structure and capabilities, which are optimized for operations in Afghanistan, to a more adaptable posture able to meet future demands. The future role of the Army has thus been defined within three core capabilities: a contingent capability for deterrence and defence; overseas engagement and capacity-building; and civil engagement and the military contribution to homeland resilience – and all from a UK-based army.

This Sapper from 9 Para Sqn RE (note the Pegasus 'zap patch' below the jump-wings on his right sleeve) wears Multi-Terrain Pattern (MTP) combats, Osprey Mk 4 armour, and the new Mk 7 helmet; its strap to mount night-vision equipment has a Guardian Mockingbird Identification Friend or Foe (IFF) beacon attached. Note the standard PLCE and the issued goggles for this period. His L85A2 rifle retains the original Sight Unit Small Arms Trilux (SUSAT) sight.
(Crown Copyright 2011)

The result will be an army structured more for graduated readiness than for executing an enduring operation. It is therefore to have a new, integrated structure of Regulars and Reserves; it will have a clear delineation of roles by way of a 'Reaction Force', with formations and units at highest readiness, and an 'Adaptable Force' at lower readiness, all supported by 'Force Troops'. The Adaptable Force and Force Troops will also have regional responsibilities across the UK. With sufficient notice and preparation, the infantry brigades of the Adaptable Force will provide a brigade contribution to enduring stabilization operations. Clearly, however, the nature of future operations can never be predicted for certain, and organizing, equipping and training the Army for what *might* happen are constant challenges, with all operational commitments having major effects on all peacetime assumptions.

Character

The British Army has a character very much of its own, despite the many changes over the centuries. For the greater part of its history it has been an all-volunteer force, and its strength has been underpinned by the so-called 'regimental system', of which more later. The Army's position in society remains ambiguous, as immortalized long ago in Rudyard Kipling's poem 'Tommy': Tommy Atkins – the British soldier – has been highly regarded in war, but invariably less so in peacetime. The unpopularity at home of the wars in Iraq and Afghanistan has not made the Army itself any less popular – indeed, the public has rallied to support its soldiers in ways not previously seen since 1945.

In an attempt to enshrine government support in actual legislation a 'military covenant' has been created, laying out for the first time the country's legal commitment to supporting its Service personnel in return for their commitment and sacrifice. (In referring to the soldier the public and the press continue to hang on to the term 'squaddie', something of a legacy of the post-1945 generation of National Service conscripts; it is not used within the Army, where 'Tom' is the common term of endearment and respect, with its obvious link to Kipling.)

The Army modernizes constantly, and goes to great lengths to keep up with the times while maintaining the fundamentals of military capability and discipline. So, in addition to the various structural changes over the years, the Army has also embraced a number of institutional changes. While institutional racism was a fairly inconspicuous but nevertheless unpalatable reality some decades ago, great strides were made subsequently to achieve racial equality, marked finally by the recruitment of black and Asian soldiers into the Household Division. Equality for women was initiated with the disbandment of the Women's Royal Army Corps (WRAC) in 1992, with all female soldiers henceforward being recruited directly into other regiments and corps. Their employment is still restricted, officially, to non-frontline roles, although this is more realistically defined as non-participation in dismounted close combat. But while women are not allowed to join armoured or infantry regiments, the deployment in Afghanistan of, for example, female helicopter pilots, artillery and engineer officers renders the restriction somewhat illusory.

There is some controversy over the number of troops born overseas. In 2012, for example, foreign-born soldiers, including the 3,680-strong Brigade of Gurkhas, constituted a record 12 per cent of manpower. Around 38 countries in addition to Nepal are represented in the Army, all except Eire being Commonwealth countries. Most such personnel are from Africa and the Caribbean, but with around 2,200 Fiji provides the highest single number, and there are over 800 South Africans and 800 Ghanaians.

Composition

Over the past 25 years radical structural changes have occurred from top to bottom of the Army. This book must necessarily track these changes, linking them to the Army of today – 'today' being defined as 2013, but, given the continuing transition towards 2020, the term is something of a moving target. The Army has long comprised two 'armies' within it: the full-time component, known as the Regular Army or Regulars; and the part-time component, known as the Territorial Army (TA) or Territorials, and now increasingly identified as Reserves. While officialdom has long attempted to call this 'One Army', Army 2020 will actually see the full integration of the Regulars and the Reserves within a single force structure.

Nomenclature

A word on the British Army's idiosyncratic nomenclature, and some definition of terms, are necessary for the sake of civilian and overseas readers, since many of the terms used have come to have, over the passage of many years, confusingly different meanings depending upon the context. The essential distinction to grasp is between 'administrative' identities and 'operational' identities, the latter used in this context to mean the groupings in which troops are assembled to actually deploy and fight. (Any reader who is completely unfamiliar with this world may find it easiest to think of the administrative identity as a 'family' of soldiers usually wearing the same cap badge, and the operational identities as the 'employers' to which different family members disperse for work.)

A 'formation' is defined as a brigade, division, or higher. A 'unit' is an infantry battalion or a cavalry or artillery regiment, which are of roughly similar size, and are comparable when referred to in an operational sense. The definition is not helped by the fact that administrative infantry 'regiments' may contain either a number of operational battalions or, in some cases, only one. (Another type of temporary tactical unit is the battlegroup, which is discussed below under 'The Army on Operations and at War'.) A 'sub-unit' is a company, squadron or battery within an infantry, cavalry or artillery unit.

The meanings of the terms 'corps' and 'division' also differ depending on context. In the operational context a corps is a fighting formation made up of a number of fighting divisions. In this sense the Army retains one 'fighting' corps headquarters, albeit in its guise as the NATO ACE (Allied Command Europe) Rapid Reaction Corps (ARRC). Other than that, 'corps' means an entirely administrative structure governing certain arms and services, such as, for example, the Royal Armoured Corps or the Royal Logistic Corps, and should be viewed as part of the Army's wider system of 'regimental families'.

In addition to the operational divisions, and the divisional organization that was present within the UK up until 2012, the infantry also sits within a wholly separate framework of 'administrative' divisions (titled Queen's, King's, etc) under Headquarters Infantry. Headquarters Royal Armoured Corps exercises a similar role over all the cavalry and tank regiments, but the Household Cavalry and the regiments of Foot Guards sit within their own administrative headquarters – the Household Division. The Royal Regiment of Artillery has its own rules, in that it is akin to one of the administrative corps and its subordinate tactical units are all designated as 'regiments' – though all Gunners are proud members of one 'Regiment'.

Indistinguishable from his Regular counterpart: a Territorial soldier from 4th Bn Mercian Regt in Afghanistan, sporting the sleeve flash of the regiment's cap badge in black on a pale khaki diamond. This battalion has had more soldiers deployed on operations than any other Territorial unit. The 7.62mm General Purpose Machine Gun (GPMG) is still used for close combat despite its weight and the ready availability of the handier 5.56mm Minimi; it is also particularly effective when tripod-mounted in the sustained-fire role. (4 Mercian)

Strengths

In 2000 Regular strength was about 109,500 personnel, plus about 3,800 Gurkhas. Reductions resulting from FAS 2004 brought that Regular strength down to some 102,000. The most dramatic reduction of all will result from SDSR 2010, bringing Regular strength down to 82,000 by 2018.

The TA's current constitution is defined under the Reserve Forces Act 1996. It contains three main categories, of which Group A are the headquarters and units providing the national reserve, which can be employed at home or overseas. Between 2000 and 2012 the TA was whittled away from a figure of about 51,000 to some 19,000 personnel. Army 2020 declares that the total number of available forces will be 'rebalanced', and the loss of so many Regulars will be compensated for by creating a larger number of 'Reserve Forces' at 30,000 (although the 'Future Reserves' plan sees the total number of major units reduced from 71 to 68 by 2016). The Territorials have more than proved themselves over lengthy operational deployments; 3,861 TA soldiers served in the 2003 invasion of Iraq alone.

The Army also maintains the Regular Army Reserve. This constitutes various categories, depending mainly on length of Regular service and age. The basic principle is that all ex-Regular soldiers have a reserve liability and can be subject to compulsory recall. Since 1997, all soldiers remain on the

General Sir David Richards GCB, CBE, DSO, ADC Gen, Chief of the Defence Staff 2009–2013 and previously Chief of the General Staff. Commissioned into the Royal Artillery, he wears the general officers' cap badge on the RA's dark blue beret, a windproof smock in MTP camouflage with a rank slide on the upwards-buttoning chest strap, and an old 58 Pattern webbing belt.
(Crown Copyright 2012)

Regular Reserve or Long Term Reserve for 18 years from the date of completion of their full-time service or until the age of 55. In 2003, 251 recalled Regular Reservists were deployed for the invasion of Iraq.

Mention must also be made of the cadet forces. The Army Cadet Force is a national voluntary youth organization and, while not part of the Army, is sponsored by it. It has more than 1,700 detachments across 57 counties, and is an important source of recruits for the Army. In addition, the Combined Cadet Forces in the (largely) private school sector include Army detachments.

Higher command

The head of the armed forces is the reigning monarch, but direct command, control and management are provided by the Ministry of Defence (MoD). At its head sits the Secretary of State for Defence. He is assisted by two principal advisers: the Permanent Secretary, a civil servant, and the Chief of the Defence Staff (CDS), the officer who is the professional head of the armed forces. This post is rotated between the three armed services, and when held by an Army officer it used to be filled by a field marshal. That rank was suspended in peacetime in 1997, and the post has since been held by a four-star general or the equivalent in the Royal Navy or Royal Air Force. The professional head of the Army is the Chief of the General Staff (CGS), another four-star appointment. The Army is governed by the Army Board, which is chaired by the Secretary of State, although CGS chairs his own Executive Committee of the Army Board (ECAB).

Away from the top-level headquarters, the Field Army was once divided between two four-star headquarters: Headquarters United Kingdom Land Forces (HQ UKLF) at Wilton in Wiltshire, and Headquarters British Army of the Rhine (BAOR) at Rheindahlen in West Germany. There were additional overseas garrisons, including until 1997 a substantial commitment to Hong Kong.

A **CEREMONIAL DRESS**

Ceremonial dress – Full Dress – is commonly worn in the Household Division but, with the exception of bands and other 'music', far less so elsewhere in the Army.

1: Captain, Royal Gibraltar Regiment; Full Dress, 2012

An unusual instance is the Royal Gibraltar Regiment, of which this captain is shown during public duties in London in 2012. He wears typical infantry Full Dress as originally laid down in 1881 Regulations, but with a white helmet unique to this regiment, and its limestone-grey facing colour on the cuffs and collar rather than the blue of other Royal regiments. Lace and piping on the cuffs are also simplified, but, while the RG is a late 20th-century creation, all other uniform details and the 1895 Pattern infantry officers' sword would have been recognized in Queen Victoria's army.

2: Lieutenant, Light Dragoons; No. 1 Dress, 2013

Number 1 Dress is worn more universally for important ceremonial duties, although this lieutenant of the Light Dragoons is dressed as his regiment's duty officer of the day. His 'blue patrols' are fairly standard for line cavalry officers – the tunic with chain-mail epaulettes, and overalls with cavalry yellow stripes – but with notable regimental distinctions. In addition to regimental badges and buttons, this officer wears a regimental shoulder-belt of silver and gold lace mounted on crimson leather. Most distinctive are the silver ornaments of an Austrian crown and regimental battle honours, with a pair of ornamental spikes that hark back to the days when light cavalry were employed to spike enemy guns.

3: Private, Balaklava Company, Royal Regiment of Scotland; No. 1 Dress, 2014

Number 1 Dress for Scottish soldiers is represented here by a private from Balaklava Coy 5 SCOTS, a purely ceremonial sub-unit. All soldiers of the Royal Regiment of Scotland wear a universal pattern of uniform with Glengarry bonnet, doublet in Archer green, and kilt of Government 1A (Sutherland) pattern in green and black. **(3a)** shows detail of the regimental collar badge. Note the green nylon covers fitted for ceremonial occasions to the SA80 rifle; it is carried here at the 'shoulder arms' position, which can be on either the right or left side.

The major reductions and reorganizations that resulted from the effective end of the Cold War saw the closure of HQ BAOR in March 1994.

Command of the Field Army was brought together at Wilton in April 1995, when HQ UKLF was renamed Headquarters Land Command. Between 1995 and 2008, CGS governed the Army through three subordinate headquarters: Land Command, responsible for operational command of about 75 per cent of the Army's manpower; Adjutant General's Branch, responsible for personnel, individual training, doctrine and administration; and Equipment Support (Land). Following FAS 2004, HQ Land Command became HQ Land Forces in 2008 and moved to Andover in 2009.

Finally (at least for the purposes of this book), the various Army staffs were amalgamated in November 2011 into a single staff working out of Army Headquarters at Marlborough Lines, Andover. CGS now commands through three subordinate three-stars (lieutenant generals): Commander Land Forces (CLF), the Adjutant General, and Commander Force Development & Training, with CLF now *primus inter pares* as CGS's deputy and holding, from 2011, effective command of the whole of the British Army's fighting capability. Command during actual operations will usually be devolved to a deployed joint force commander, but this is complemented by Army Headquarters' role of delivering and sustaining the Army's operational capability. To achieve this CLF had, up to 2013, nine subordinate commands, as shown in **Table 1**. However, Army 2020 will see further restructuring and renaming.

LAND FORCES STRUCTURE

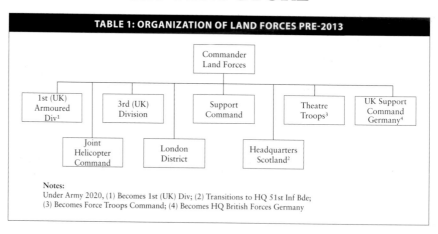

TABLE 1: ORGANIZATION OF LAND FORCES PRE-2013

Commander Land Forces

1st (UK) Armoured Div[1] — 3rd (UK) Division — Support Command — Theatre Troops[3] — UK Support Command Germany[4]

Joint Helicopter Command — London District — Headquarters Scotland[2]

Notes:
Under Army 2020, (1) Becomes 1st (UK) Div; (2) Transitions to HQ 51st Inf Bde; (3) Becomes Force Troops Command; (4) Becomes HQ British Forces Germany

With reference to Table 1, it is important to detail the actual structure of Land Forces, and to note the differences between the Army pre- and post-SDSR 2010, and the consequences of the Army 2020 programme. A distinction must also be made between the peacetime structure of Land Forces, which has a large operationally ready structure within it, and the organization of Land Forces for actual operations.

The 1990s: from BAOR to ARRC

The principal high-level fighting formation of the Cold War era was 1st (British) Corps, based for most of its life at Bielefeld in West Germany. Following the disbandment of 1st (British) Corps in 1992, the UK continued to provide the overall command structure to NATO's newly created HQ ARRC. This headquarters took over the facilities of HQ BAOR at Rheindahlen in 1994, until it moved to Innsworth in the UK in 2010. Like the other five NATO corps headquarters, HQ ARRC has no permanently assigned divisions in peacetime, but did provide the command element to operations in Bosnia in 1996 and in Kosovo in 1999, and, subsequently, in support of the International Security Assistance Force (ISAF) in Afghanistan. Should HQ ARRC deploy in a general war setting it is likely that its assigned subordinate formations would include a good part of UK Land Forces.

At the time of Options 1990 the 'ready' element of the Army contained 1st Corps with four subordinate divisions, three of them armoured (1st, 3rd and 4th) based in Germany and an infantry division (2nd) based in the UK. 1st and 4th Armd Divs each contained three armoured brigades (7th, 12th & 22nd, and 11th, 20th & 33rd, respectively). 3rd Armd Div had two armoured brigades (4th & 6th) and the UK-based 19th Inf Bde; and 2nd Inf Div had one Regular brigade (24th) and two Territorial brigades (15th & 49th). At the same time UKLF contained three independent brigades (1st & 2nd Inf Bdes and 5th Airborne Bde). The Northern Ireland command had two, later increased (for the second time) to three infantry brigades (3rd, 8th & 39th), although most of its units were on short operational tours, having been assigned from other formations. The TA also contained four infantry brigades (43rd, 51st, 52nd & 54th) organized primarily for home defence. Headquarters 2nd Inf Div and 4th Armd Div were disbanded in 1992 and 1993 respectively, with the various brigade headquarters being reduced as described later.

Home garrison

In the mid-1990s the UK's home garrison was reorganized, the old districts being placed in a new regional structure under HQ Regional Forces. Commander Regional Forces had under him four regional 'regenerative' formations: HQ 2nd Div in Edinburgh, HQ 4th Div in Aldershot, HQ 5th Div in Shrewsbury, and HQ London District. These contained between them 11 regional brigades and all of the UK garrisons (see **Table 2**). The brigades in turn contained the majority of TA units and a number of Regular units not assigned to operational formations. Thus all UK-based units, whether or not

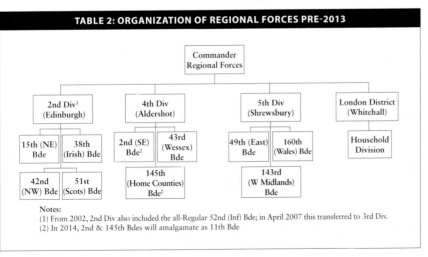

TABLE 2: ORGANIZATION OF REGIONAL FORCES PRE-2013

Commander Regional Forces

- 2nd Div[1] (Edinburgh)
  - 15th (NE) Bde
  - 38th (Irish) Bde
  - 42nd (NW) Bde
  - 51st (Scots) Bde
- 4th Div (Aldershot)
  - 2nd (SE) Bde[2]
  - 43rd (Wessex) Bde
  - 145th (Home Counties) Bde[2]
- 5th Div (Shrewsbury)
  - 49th (East) Bde
  - 160th (Wales) Bde
  - 143rd (W Midlands) Bde
- London District (Whitehall)
  - Household Division

Notes:
(1) From 2002, 2nd Div also included the all-Regular 52nd (Inf) Bde; in April 2007 this transferred to 3rd Div.
(2) In 2014, 2nd & 145th Bdes will amalgamate as 11th Bde

part of the operational structure, were administered by these formations. London District commands all units located within the M25 motorway; its primary function is ceremonial, and GOC London is also therefore the Major General Commanding the Household Division.

Northern Ireland

Not shown in either table is HQ Northern Ireland, which commanded all formations and units assigned to the Province. For much of its existence it comprised the three Regular infantry brigades mentioned above plus one TA brigade, 107th (Ulster). As the Troubles diminished, units were gradually withdrawn and the operational structure was drawn down. 39th Inf Bde absorbed 3rd Inf Bde in September 2004 and 8th Inf Bde in September 2006. In December 2006, 39th Bde merged with 107th Bde, being retitled 38th (Irish) Bde in August 2007, and combining at the same time with the remnants of HQ Northern Ireland. The latter was formally dissolved in January 2009, 38th Bde then being placed under HQ 2nd Division.

Restructuring post-SDSR 2010

Following SDSR 2010, the entire regional organization was restructured in order to support the changes required for Army 2020. This includes the concept of the UK as the 'firm base' within which regional forces continue to support the Army's nationwide responsibilities, but at the same time being better organized to sustain and support commands deployed on operations.

Headquarters Regional Forces was thus disbanded in January 2012; it was replaced by HQ Support Command, with responsibility for all remaining regional forces outside London District, and a separate HQ Scotland. These were all two-star headquarters, and can be identified in Table 1. The regenerative divisional headquarters were then also disbanded: 4th Div in January 2012; 2nd and 5th Divs in April 2012. In 2013 HQ Support Command drew down to a two-star formation, responsible for running all remaining regional brigades. As such it will also absorb HQ Scotland when that becomes HQ 51st Infantry Brigade.

Outside the UK, UK Support Command Germany did a similar job to HQ Support Command. It was set up in Rheindahlen on the disbandment of HQ BAOR in 1994, and in 2013 it was renamed HQ British Forces Germany and moved to Bielefeld. It provides administrative and infrastructure support to what remains of the Army estate in Germany. Both HQ Support Command and HQ BFG will disband on the establishment of HQ 1st Div in the UK, and the final withdrawal from Germany.

The Army also retains a significant, if reduced, presence in overseas garrisons, training units and training and advisory teams. There are four remaining garrisons: Falkland Islands, Gibraltar, Cyprus and Brunei (Belize having closed in 2011). Brunei is home to an important jungle training school, and the Army carries out training

British Army Training Unit Kenya provides key pre-operational training for units deploying to Afghanistan; here a section from 1st Bn Princess of Wales's Royal Regt fight through a trench system during Exercise 'Askari Thunder' in 2011. They are equipped with sensors for Tactical Engagement Simulation training, with blank-firing attachments and laser units on their rifles. Once they arrive in Afghanistan all troops must then complete Reception, Staging and Onward Integration (RSOI) exercises before conducting operations. (1 PWRR)

exercises in a number of foreign countries on a regular basis. For example, Poland has hosted brigades and units from 1st Armd Div since the 1990s, and Jordan sees frequent training exercises for light forces. The most important operational training units are, for armoured forces especially, British Army Training Unit Suffield (BATUS) in Canada, and for light troops British Army Training Unit Kenya (BATUK). Training and advisory teams are spread around the world and are expanded or reduced as the situation dictates. In 2013 there were about 20 of these active in different countries, the most significant being in Sierra Leone, Ghana, East Africa (based in Kenya), South Africa, Oman, Saudi Arabia, the United Arab Emirates, Jordan and Mali.

Finally, it should be noted that a number of Army Commando units and sub-units are permanently assigned to 3rd Commando Bde in the Royal Navy. The principal units are 29 Cdo Regt Royal Artillery and 24 Cdo Regt Royal Engineers, although the latter will disband in 2015. Additionally, 1st Bn The Rifles became part of the Commando brigade in 2008, but will move to the Adaptive Force under Army 2020.

PEACETIME OPERATIONAL FORMATIONS

Pre-SDSR 2010
The remaining formations in Table 1 represented CLF's operational formations: 1st Armd Div, 3rd Div, Joint Helicopter Command (containing significant RN and RAF elements), and Theatre Troops, which will become Force Troops Command under Army 2020. Only the two 'ready' divisions (1st Armd and 3rd) can be described as true operational formations, capable of deploying and fighting in their own right, while the other two provide critical support and enabling activities.

In addition to the two ready divisions, in August 2008, due to the requirement to command operations in Iraq and Afghanistan simultaneously, HQ 6th Div was established in York to take its turn in Afghanistan; it was subsequently disbanded in April 2011. **Table 3** shows the two ready divisions, their subordinate brigades and the one independent brigade in Land Forces as of 2013. In addition to their brigades, each division contains a number of 'divisional troops' under direct command, including signals, engineers, aviation, military police, logistics and maintenance units.

Each of the brigades contains a number of assigned Regular units. For much of the Army's existence the units within any brigade (as well as the

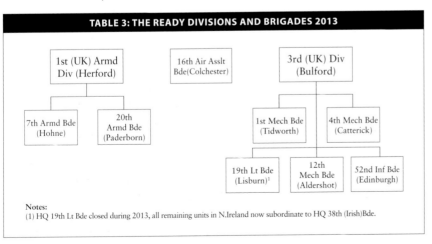

TABLE 3: THE READY DIVISIONS AND BRIGADES 2013

1st (UK) Armd Div (Herford)
- 7th Armd Bde (Hohne)
- 20th Armd Bde (Paderborn)

16th Air Asslt Bde(Colchester)

3rd (UK) Div (Bulford)
- 1st Mech Bde (Tidworth)
- 4th Mech Bde (Catterick)
- 19th Lt Bde (Lisburn)[1]
- 12th Mech Bde (Aldershot)
- 52nd Inf Bde (Edinburgh)

Notes:
(1) HQ 19th Lt Bde closed during 2013, all remaining units in N.Ireland now subordinate to HQ 38th (Irish)Bde.

Mastiff 2 (foreground) and Ridgeback protected patrol vehicles (PPVs) prepare to lead a combat logistic patrol in support of 20th Armd Bde in Afghanistan during 'Herrick XV'. Such convoys are vital for maintaining bases and operations, and all need sophisticated route clearance and protection; the task, if not the kit, would be familiar to British troops on the North-West Frontier a century ago. Under Army 2020, the 6x6 Mastiff 2 PPV will be the mount of the 'heavy protected mobility' infantry battalions; a development of the US General Dynamics Cougar, it carries two crew plus eight infantrymen. (Crown Copyright 2012)

divisional units) were subject to periodic change. While armoured, artillery and engineer regiments did move from one station to another, a typical peacetime tour for an armoured regiment in Germany was 12 years in any one brigade, and artillery and engineer regiments would stay far longer in one place. However, infantry battalions invariably moved every two to three years, although the normal tour for armoured infantry was five to six years.

The annual notification of moves of units was called the Arms Plot. This was finally stopped in 2008 to reduce the constant need to retrain units for new roles, and the great costs involved in moving soldiers and their families.

B

PARADE UNIFORM

Although parades are today often conducted in Combat Dress, No. 2 Dress is commonly worn for higher-profile events.

1: Colour Sergeant, 2nd Battalion Mercian Regiment; No. 2 Dress, 2013

This NCO represents the now standardized 'Future Army Dress' introduced in 2009. For this non-Royal regiment the regimental distinctions are, in addition to cap and collar badges and the shoulder titles, the black backing to rank badges; the special right-arm badge; and (on the left shoulder, concealed here by the rifle) a regimental lanyard in cerise, green and buff twist cord. The special arm badge **(1a)** is an example of commemorative insignia from constituent former units surviving the rounds of regimental amalgamations; the glider recalls the World War II service of the antecedent 2nd Bn South Staffordshire Regt in 1st Air-Landing Bde of 1st Airborne Div, superimposed on the Stafford knot device historically associated with Staffordshire's regiments (the old 38th, 64th and 80th Foot and Staffordshire Yeomanry). The oak-leaves in his cap show that he is on parade in front of his Colonel in Chief, the Prince of Wales. Note the rifle and fixed bayonet at the 'slope arms' position, reintroduced for the SA80 during the 1980s.

2: Lance Corporal Drummer, 2nd Battalion Princess of Wales's Royal Regiment; Full Dress, 2012

Due to operational commitments, regiments have some difficulty in keeping trained drummers, buglers and the like on establishment and kitted out in Full Dress. This side-drummer from 2 PWRR is dressed and equipped largely in accordance with 1881 Regulations. This is an example of a Royal regiment, with blue facings on collar and cuffs, and the universal pattern of crown lace on the tunic; a drum badge is worn on his upper right sleeve above the rank chevron. These uniforms and drums are expensive to maintain, largely from regimental funds, so he wears issued No. 1 Dress trousers with their broader red stripe, as opposed to the narrow-striped Full Dress trousers worn in the Foot Guards. Note on his upper left sleeve the PWRR's tiger badge **(2a)**; like **1a**, this is commemorative of an antecedent unit, in this case referring to the service in India from 1805 to 1826 of the old 67th Foot, later 2nd Bn Royal Hampshire Regiment.

3: Major, Royal Logistic Corps; Summer Service Dress

While worn largely off parade, No. 4 Dress for officers – Summer Service Dress – is a popular uniform for those who have it. This late-entry major from the Royal Logistic Corps, having risen through the ranks, demonstrates his 30-plus years' service by his chestful of medals. His forage cap has a red poppy on the left, indicating that he is attending a Remembrance service somewhere in a hot country.

2

2a

1

1a

3

Unit moves have not halted altogether, and the re-adjustments required for Army 2020 will see the remainder of the Army brought back from Germany; in the infantry alone, 16 battalions will move station.

The number and types of units in each brigade depend on its overall role. Again, it must be noted that for deployments on actual operations brigades are often restructured, as described later. Table 3 shows that in 2013 the Army had eight ready brigades of four types: armoured, mechanized, light, and air assault. Each of these types has a different structure, and those of the same type also have different combinations of units depending largely on

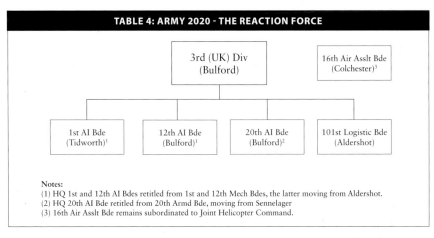

TABLE 4: ARMY 2020 - THE REACTION FORCE

3rd (UK) Div (Bulford)

16th Air Asslt Bde (Colchester)[3]

1st AI Bde (Tidworth)[1]

12th AI Bde (Bulford)[1]

20th AI Bde (Bulford)[2]

101st Logistic Bde (Aldershot)

Notes:
(1) HQ 1st and 12th AI Bdes retitled from 1st and 12th Mech Bdes, the latter moving from Aldershot.
(2) HQ 20th AI Bde retitled from 20th Armd Bde, moving from Sennelager
(3) 16th Air Asslt Bde remains subordinated to Joint Helicopter Command.

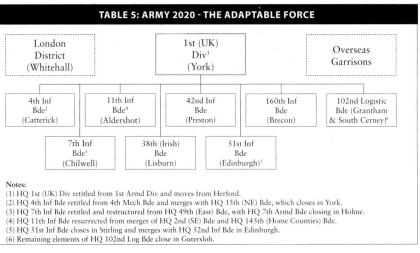

TABLE 5: ARMY 2020 - THE ADAPTABLE FORCE

London District (Whitehall)

1st (UK) Div[1] (York)

Overseas Garrisons

4th Inf Bde[2] (Catterick)

11th Inf Bde[4] (Aldershot)

42nd Inf Bde (Preston)

160th Inf Bde (Brecon)

102nd Logistic Bde (Grantham & South Cerney)[6]

7th Inf Bde[3] (Chilwell)

38th (Irish) Bde (Lisburn)

51st Inf Bde (Edinburgh)[5]

Notes:
(1) HQ 1st (UK) Div retitled from 1st Armd Div and moves from Herford.
(2) HQ 4th Inf Bde retitled from 4th Mech Bde and merges with HQ 15th (NE) Bde, which closes in York.
(3) HQ 7th Inf Bde retitled and restructured from HQ 49th (East) Bde, with HQ 7th Armd Bde closing in Hohne.
(4) HQ 11th Inf Bde resurrected from merger of HQ 2nd (SE) Bde and HQ 145th (Home Counties) Bde.
(5) HQ 51st Inf Bde closes in Stirling and merges with HQ 52nd Inf Bde in Edinburgh.
(6) Remaining elements of HQ 102nd Log Bde close in Gutersloh.

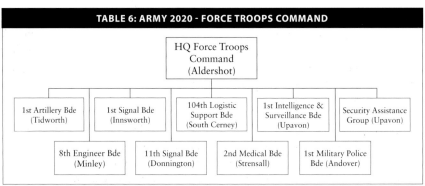

TABLE 6: ARMY 2020 - FORCE TROOPS COMMAND

HQ Force Troops Command (Aldershot)

1st Artillery Bde (Tidworth)

1st Signal Bde (Innsworth)

104th Logistic Support Bde (South Cerney)

1st Intelligence & Surveillance Bde (Upavon)

Security Assistance Group (Upavon)

8th Engineer Bde (Minley)

11th Signal Bde (Donnington)

2nd Medical Bde (Strensall)

1st Military Police Bde (Andover)

availability. (The types of units are given in detail under 'Regiments & Corps', below.) In 2008 HQ 11th Light Bde was activated at Aldershot as an additional formation headquarters for Afghanistan. It was subsequently disbanded in mid-2010, but will be resurrected in Aldershot in 2014 by the amalgamation of 2nd and 145th Brigades.

Restructuring operational formations for 'Army 2020'

All of the above is set to change radically with Army 2020, which seeks to provide an even more adaptable and flexible UK-based force, and one removed from the present optimization of structure and training for an enduring operation (i.e. Afghanistan). Graduated readiness is the objective, and the armoured infantry is to be the core capability, with tanks organized for intimate support. The three key elements are:

The **Reaction Force (see Table 4)** will provide the high-readiness forces trained and equipped to undertake short-notice contingency tasks. Predominantly Regulars, under HQ 3rd Div it will have three armoured infantry (AI) brigades stationed around the Salisbury Plain Training Area, and 16th Air Asslt Brigade. Each AI brigade will contain an armoured cavalry (recce) regiment, an armoured (main battle tank) regiment, two AI battalions, and one 'heavy protected mobility' infantry battalion. The three AI brigades will rotate through annual cycles of lead, training and other tasks, with the lead brigade providing a lead battlegroup and 16th Air Asslt Bde a lead task force at very high readiness. 101st Logistic Bde is integral, but all combat support and additional combat service support are allocated for training and operations as required.

The **Adaptable Force (see Table 5)** is a pool of Regulars and Reserves organized under HQ 1st Div, containing seven regionally-based infantry brigades and 102nd Logistic Brigade. This Force will be responsible for the Army's standing commitments to Cyprus, Brunei, the Falklands, Public Duties and the UN, for overseas military capacity-building, for support to homeland resilience, and for supporting any enduring operations. The infantry brigades will each contain a mix of light cavalry regiments, 'light protected mobility' infantry battalions and light-role infantry battalions, all paired with Reserve units.

Integral to both Forces is **HQ Force Troops Command** and its constituent brigades (see Table 6).

THE REGIMENTS & CORPS

The organization and roles of the regiments and corps of the Army are complicated by the historical basis of the structure as a whole, of each arm and service, and of each regiment and corps. This chapter describes the organization and roles in peacetime as of 2013, noting all preceding changes since 1990, and the changes to be enacted under Army 2020.

The Army remains wedded to the ethos of the 'regimental system' – a unique historical structure that might be criticized for a degree of parochialism and lack of cohesion above the regimental level, but whose strength is also greater than the sum of its parts. The system has endured constant change, as this book testifies, but it has proven strength within it, which lies at the heart of the Army's fighting power. It has meant that the soldier continues to identify

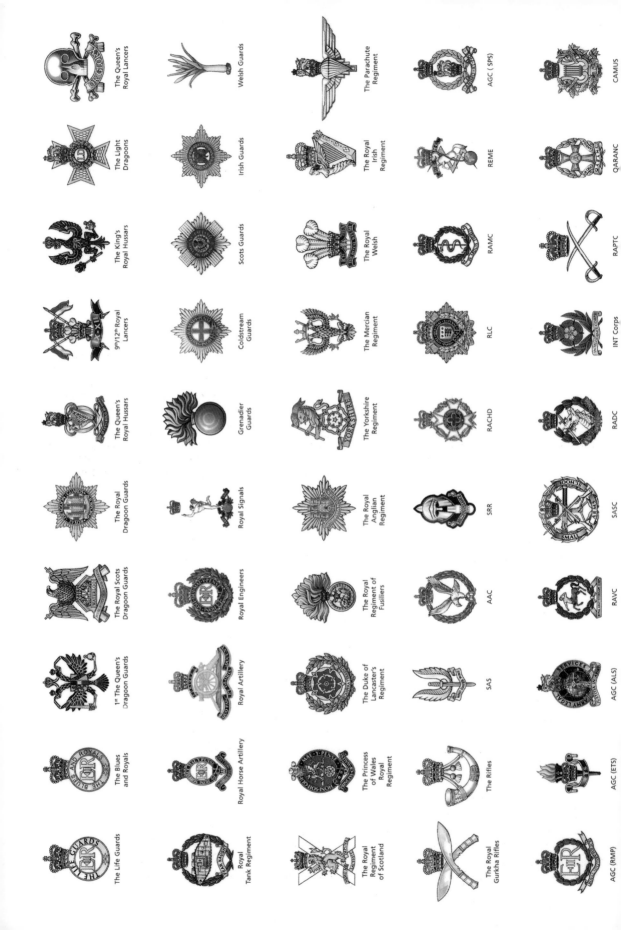

The Queen's Royal Lancers	Welsh Guards	The Parachute Regiment	AGC (SPS)	CAMUS
The Light Dragoons	Irish Guards	The Royal Irish Regiment	REME	QARANC
The King's Royal Hussars	Scots Guards	The Royal Welsh	RAMC	RAPTC
9th/12th Royal Lancers	Coldstream Guards	The Mercian Regiment	RLC	INT Corps
The Queen's Royal Hussars	Grenadier Guards	The Yorkshire Regiment	RACHD	RADC
The Royal Dragoon Guards	Royal Signals	The Royal Anglian Regiment	SRR	SASC
The Royal Scots Dragoon Guards	Royal Engineers	The Royal Regiment of Fusiliers	AAC	RAVC
1st The Queen's Dragoon Guards	Royal Artillery	The Duke of Lancaster's Regiment	SAS	AGC (ALS)
The Blues and Royals	Royal Horse Artillery	The Princess of Wales's Royal Regiment	The Rifles	AGC (ETS)
The Life Guards	Royal Tank Regiment	The Royal Regiment of Scotland	The Royal Gurkha Rifles	AGC (RMP)

far more readily with his regiment or corps (his 'cap badge') than with any brigade or division to which his unit is assigned. That may change as a result of Army 2020, which will see units become more permanently assigned than ever before to higher, combined-arms formations.

Regimental tradition – which is as relevant to the corps as it is to the actual regiments – lies at the core of the system. Great efforts are made to preserve these traditions as far as possible through every period of change. While those serving and the veterans alike might mourn the loss of their old title and badge, there is certainly no hint of diminished capability as a result. The new badge is soon accepted (particularly after the first operational tour), and becomes as sacred to its wearers as the badges of their forbears had been. Even when units require major reinforcement during an operation, and the reinforced unit's cap badge is therefore diluted by in-comers, the reinforcements from other regiments and corps quickly become wedded to their new family.

Iraq, 2004: Challenger 2 main battle tank of the Queen's Royal Lancers in Basrah. Despite their size, Challengers were retained in south-east Iraq for use during the insurgency that began in 2004 following the invasion the previous year. Three regiments of Challenger 2, each with 56 tanks, will equip the armoured regiments of Army 2020. (Crown Copyright 2004)

Before Options 1990 the Army categorized all regiments and corps as belonging either to the 'arms' or the 'services'. The arms were further divided between 'teeth arms' (the armour and infantry) and 'support arms' (the artillery, engineers and aviation). The services were defined as all of those corps that supported the arms. Today, all are more clearly categorized in three ways: combat units (armour, infantry and aviation); combat support units (artillery, engineers and signals); and combat service support (CSS) units, which comprise all the logistic and administrative elements. The order of precedence of all regiments and corps is decided largely, but not invariably, by the date of formation of the original antecedent unit since the 1660s.

Anyone comparing today's list with that of pre-Options 1990 will notice a number of missing cap badges and a number of new ones, and this is explained below. For brevity, except where necessary the definite article ('The') is not used in these lists of titles. Many regiments also bear additional traditional titles, and these too are omitted here.

HOUSEHOLD CAVALRY & ROYAL ARMOURED CORPS

Although grouped together in what may loosely be described as the 'tank arm' of the Army, these are two distinct corps. All of the regiments that comprise the Household Cavalry and Royal Armoured Corps have entirely separate regimental distinctions, but all are grouped under the RAC for administrative purposes. In 2013 the Regular regiments had two main roles: armoured (equipped with Challenger 2 main battle tanks), and formation reconnaissance (equipped with Scimitar, CVR(T)). The RAC also includes four formed TA regiments of Yeomanry.

Army 2020 will reorganize the regiments into three types: armoured (with Challenger 2 MBT); and, in the formation reconnaissance role for Reaction Force and Adaptable Force brigades respectively, armoured cavalry and light cavalry. Armoured cavalry will initially retain CVR(T), to be replaced with

OPPOSITE
The cap badges of the Regular Army's Regiments and Corps in 2013, in order of precedence.

General Dynamics Scout, part of the Future Rapid Effects System; light cavalry will have Jackal, and lighter utility vehicles. The listing of regiments shows their current role, followed by their future Army 2020 role and brigade in brackets:

Household Cavalry
Created in 1991 from a grouping of The Life Guards and The Blues and Royals. Both are represented in equal part in the regiment's two units:

Household Cavalry Regt (HCR) Formation reconnaissance (armoured cavalry, 1st AI Bde)

Household Cavalry Mounted Regt (HCMR) Mounted ceremonial, London District

Line Cavalry & Royal Tank Regiment
The line cavalry comprises eight regiments, reducing to seven under Army 2020:

1st The Queen's Dragoon Guards (QDG) Formation reconnaissance (light cavalry, 7th Bde)

Royal Scots Dragoon Guards (SCOTS DG) Armoured (light cavalry, 51st Bde)

Royal Dragoon Guards (RDG) Formed in 1992 from 4th/7th Royal Dragoon Guards and 5th Royal Inniskilling Dragoon Guards; armoured (armoured cavalry, 20th AI Bde)

Queen's Royal Hussars (QRH) Formed in 1993 from Queen's Own Hussars and Queen's Royal Irish Hussars. Armoured (armoured, 20th AI Bde)

9th/12th Royal Lancers (9/12L) Formation reconnaissance; by 2015 amalgamates with Queen's Royal Lancers to form Royal Lancers (armoured cavalry, 12th AI Bde)

King's Royal Hussars (KRH) Formed in 1992 from Royal Hussars and 14th/20th King's Hussars. Armoured (armoured, 12th AI Bde)

Light Dragoons (LD) Formed in 1992 from 13th/18th Royal Hussars and 15th/19th King's Royal Hussars. Formation reconnaissance (light cavalry, 4th Bde)

Queen's Royal Lancers (QRL) Formed in 1993 from 16th/5th Queen's Royal Lancers and 17th/21st Lancers; formation reconnaissance (see 9th/12th Royal Lancers above)

Pre-Options 1990 there were four 'regiments' within the **Royal Tank Regt** – (1, 2, 3 and 4 RTR). These units were merged into 1 and 2 RTR in 1992 by amalgamation of, respectively, 1st & 4th Regts and 2nd & 3rd. While 2 RTR retained its armoured role, 1 RTR lost its purely armoured status when it became, with elements of the Royal Yeomanry and RAF Regt, part of the new Joint Nuclear Biological & Chemical Regt in 1999; this was retitled the Joint Chemical, Biological, Radiological & Nuclear Regt in 2005. This regiment was disbanded in 2011, with all CBRN activities transferred to the RAF. Throughout this time 1 RTR retained

Afghanistan, 2011: Scimitars – Combat Vehicles Reconnaissance (Tracked) – of 9th/12th Lancers providing route protection. CVR(T) has been the mainstay of formation reconnaissance regiments for 40 years, but the Mk 2 shown here is provided with significant enhancements in design and armour to resist improvised explosive devices (IEDs), including L-ROD bar armour and the turret-mounted counter-IED array.
(Crown Copyright 2011)

one armoured squadron at the Warminster Training Centre. (Under Army 2020, 1 RTR returns to the armoured role, but by 2015 will amalgamate with 2 RTR, being assigned to 1st AI Brigade.)

Yeomanry

All of the old Territorial regiments of Yeomanry cavalry are represented in some way in the Army. In addition to the four formed regiments, all containing squadrons drawn from a number of antecedent regiments, all of the other Yeomanry regiments are represented in the Territorial RA, RE, R SIGNALS, infantry, AAC, RLC and AMS. The organization and roles of the 'in-role' regiments are:

Afghanistan, 2009: Jackal Mobility Weapons Mounted Installation Kit (MWMIK), introduced from 2008 along with Coyote, its six-wheeled brother, to replace vulnerable Land Rover Snatch and WMIKs. This Jackal mounts a forward-facing GPMG and a rear-mounted 40mm automatic grenade-launcher. Under Army 2020, Jackal and similar light vehicles will equip Adaptable Force light cavalry reconnaissance units. (Crown Copyright 2009)

Royal Yeomanry (RY) Formed in 1967 from five antecedent Yeomanry regiments (Royal Wiltshire, Leicestershire & Derbyshire, Kent & Sharpshooters, Sherwood Rangers, Inns of Court & City). The regiment re-roled from medium reconnaissance to NBC Defence in 1996. On formation of the Joint NBC Regt in 1999, two squadrons of the RY were assigned as NBC Reserves, while the remaining three became Challenger 2 Reserve squadrons. From 2006 all five squadrons provided CBRN reconnaissance as part of the Joint CBRN Regiment. (The 2020 designation is Reserve light cavalry in 7th Brigade.)

Royal Wessex Yeomanry (RWY) Formed in 1971 by amalgamation of the Royal Wiltshire Yeomanry, Gloucestershire Hussars and Royal Devon Yeomanry, the new regiment received its own Royal title in 1979. In July 1999 it merged with the Dorset Yeomanry and took on the role of Challenger 2 crew replacement. (The 2020 designation is Reserve armoured in the Reaction Force.)

Royal Mercian & Lancastrian Yeomanry (RMLY) Formed in 1992 from the Queen's Own Mercian Yeomanry (representing the old Staffordshire, Warwickshire, Worcestershire, Shropshire and Cheshire units and the

Afghanistan, 2009: Viking armoured vehicles of 2nd Royal Tank Regt under fire. Viking was first used by the Royal Marines in 2006; while particularly useful in difficult terrain, it began to be replaced with Warthog in 2012. (Crown Copyright 2009)

Herefordshire Light Infantry) and Duke of Lancaster's Own Yeomanry; in 1999 a squadron of the Queen's Own Yeomanry was absorbed. Current role is to provide trained replacement tank crewmen for the Regular Army. (Army 2020 will break up the RMLY. Its squadrons will move to the other Yeomanry regiments, while its Headquarters will be assigned to 51st Bde and renamed HQ Scottish & North Irish Yeomanry.)

Queen's Own Yeomanry (QOY) Formed in 1971 as 2nd Armd Car Regt from five Yeomanry regiments (Ayrshire, North Irish Horse, Fife & Forfar and Scottish Horse, Northumberland Hussars, Yorkshire), all represented in its five squadrons. It has maintained the armoured reconnaissance role. (Its 2020 designation is Reserve light cavalry in 4th Brigade.)

ROYAL REGIMENT OF ARTILLERY

The Royal Artillery (RA) – the artillery 'corps' of the Army, and known as the Gunners – has, since the 1990s, assumed surveillance and target acquisition (STA) roles in addition to its traditional fire support tasks. The sub-unit of a regiment is a battery, and the loyalty of a Gunner is largely to the battery first and regiment second. The batteries all bear historical names in a very complex mixture of letters, numbers, titles and battle honours. For example, 1 RHA includes A Battery (The Chestnut Troop); 12 RA includes 12 (Minden) Battery; and 16 RA includes 30 Battery (Roger's Company).

The operational emphasis was for many years on the 'heavy' end of artillery: large-calibre tracked self-propelled guns, multi-barrelled rocket-launchers, and air defence. While this capability has been maintained in part, the requirement to fight the wars in Iraq and Afghanistan has seen the mothballing of some heavier weapons and some re-equipping with lighter calibre towed artillery.

Field regiments, now re-designated as close support (CS) regiments, are equipped with the 155mm AS90 tracked self-propelled gun or the 105mm L118 towed Light Gun. All AS90 regiments are routinely retrained on the Light Gun prior to redeployment to Afghanistan. CS regiments include the

C **BARRACK, MESS & WORKING DRESS**

1: Captain, 22nd (Cheshire) Regiment; Barrack Dress, pre-2007

One of five senior line regiments that had never been amalgamated before Future Infantry Structure took effect, the 22nd (Cheshires) were unique in officially retaining their old pre-1881 number in their title. Barrack Dress is worn infrequently, and soldiers associate it with office and staff jobs. This captain of the Cheshires prior to their amalgamation into the Mercian Regiment in 2007 is in No. 13 Dress or 'Pullover Order', wearing his regiment's cerise-coloured pullover and regimental sidehat. Every regiment and corps has its own distinctive pullover for officers and warrant officers and its own sidehat or similar, the distinctions further augmented by regimental canes or, for the cavalry, whips.

2: Staff Sergeant, Royal Engineers; Mess Dress

Mess Dress is also maintained for regimental dinners and special evening occasions in respective officers' and sergeants' messes. This RE sergeant wears his corps' No. 10 Dress, a relatively unelaborate version but demonstrating a typical 1936 Pattern jacket for a senior NCO. Note the gold lace rank chevrons on the right arm, the RE collar badges (**2a**), a diver's gold personal qualification badge on the left forearm (**2b**), and miniature medals. These are typical for a long-service senior NCO: General Service Medal with clasp 'Northern Ireland'; Gulf War Medal; Operational Service Medal with clasp 'Afghanistan'; Queen's Silver Jubilee Medal and Queen's Golden Jubilee Medal; and Accumulated Campaign Service Medal.

3: Lance Bombardier, King's Troop Royal Horse Artillery; Working Dress

The daily working dress worn by this young female lance bombardier of the King's Troop RHA indicates that she will be practising with the horsed gun teams. 'Working Dress' is something of a misnomer but continues to denote fatigue uniform of some type, here with issue riding boots, breeches and helmet. The King's Troop has also retained the green Jersey, Heavy Wool for such work, with reinforced forearms and shoulders, and shoulder straps bearing the regimental title (**3a**). The RHA's stable belt is worn over it, fastened by two buckled leather straps on the left side.

3

2a

UBIQUE

1

2

3a

RHA

2b

The 155mm AS90 tracked self-propelled gun replaced elderly Abbots and M109s in the 1990s, and has since been the Army's main close support artillery piece. Its role has been slightly eclipsed by the need for lighter weapons in Afghanistan, but three AS90 regiments will be maintained in Army 2020. (Crown Copyright)

Royal Horse Artillery (RHA), an historical title that has nothing to do with its modern role (although the RHA also includes the King's Troop, an entirely ceremonial battery equipped with horse-drawn 13-pdr guns of Great War vintage). Depth-fire regiments are equipped with the Guided Multi-Launch Rocket System (GMLRS). The air defence and STA roles are combined in some regiments. Air defence equipment comprises the Rapier low-level missile system and the Starstreak High Velocity Missile (HVM). STA units are equipped with an array of ground-based and aerial STA systems, including unmanned aerial vehicles (UAVs).

Prior to Options 1990 there were 23 Regular artillery regiments of all types plus six regiments in the TA. Options 1990 reduced this to 17 Regular regiments, and in 1998 a seventh Territorial regiment was resurrected. One Rapier-equipped air defence regiment (22) was disbanded in 2004, and a number of regiments have been re-roled as required.

In 2013, five CS regiments (1 RHA, 3 RHA, 4 RA, 19 RA & 26 RA) were equipped with AS90, and three (7 Para RHA, 29 Cdo RA & 40 RA) with the Light Gun; 40 RA will be disbanded at the end of 2015. 5 RA's role is STA only, while two regiments remain dedicated to air defence (12 RA, with HVM and additional STA roles, and 16 RA with Rapier). 32 RA and 47 RA are both equipped with UAVs. The one remaining GMLRS regiment (39) also disbands at the end of 2015, from which point the remaining AS90 regiments will each receive one GMLRS battery. 14 RA continues in the training role at the Royal School of Artillery, and the King's Troop RHA (see above) remains in service for ceremonial duties.

Following the major restructuring of the TA in 2006 the seven remaining volunteer artillery regiments were reorganized. Three (100, 103 & 105 RA) are equipped with the Light Gun; 101 RA with GMLRS; 104 RA with UAVs; and 106 RA with HVM. The seventh regiment is the Honourable Artillery Company (HAC), which has an STA and covert observation-post role. 100 RA will disband under the Future Reserves plan.

Regular regiments have usually been allocated to parent brigades, but under Army 2020 only one CS regiment (7 RHA in 16th Air Asslt Bde) will retain this attachment, along with 29 RA in 3rd Commando Brigade. The majority will move to Force Troops Command. CS regiments and three Reserve regiments (101, 103 & 105 RA) will come under 1st Artillery Bde, and all STA and UAV regiments will go to 1st Intelligence & Surveillance Brigade. The two Regular and one Reserve air defence regiments will be assigned to the new Joint Ground Based Air Defence Command under the RAF.

CORPS OF ROYAL ENGINEERS

The Royal Engineers (RE), known as the Sappers, provide combat engineering and a wide array of military and conventional engineering requirements, as well as some specialist tasks such as explosive ordnance disposal (EOD) and search, and diving. HQRE is at Chatham, and the Corps' training establishment is the Royal School of Military Engineering, which is divided between training schools at Chatham, Minley and Melton Mowbray.

When the Army was focused largely on operations in North-West Europe, military engineering was biased heavily towards the provision of armoured engineers and bridging equipment for the armoured divisions. Iraq and Afghanistan have demanded different Sapper efforts, but, whatever the task, Sappers have continued to maintain three principal roles: mobility support, e.g. providing means to cross obstacles and bridge rivers; counter-mobility, to deny enemy movement, e.g. laying minefields; and protection, e.g. constructing field defences.

RE regiments are equipped according to their role. For many years armoured engineering suffered limitations due to obsolete equipment, with vehicles based on aged Centurion and Chieftain tank chassis (known throughout the Army as the 'antiques roadshow') supporting the armoured divisions. A major modernization programme has seen the introduction since 2007 of a number of new equipments. These include the Trojan, a Challenger 2 MBT-based Armoured Vehicle Royal Engineers (AVRE); the Titan Armoured Vehicle Launched Bridge (AVLB); and the Terrier General Support Engineer Vehicle. In addition to the Close Support Bridges mounted on AVLBs, the Bridge 1990 (BR90) series includes the General Support Bridge, which uses the Automated Bridge Launching Equipment (ABLE); the Medium Girder Bridge; the Logistic Support Bridge; and the Air Portable Ferry Bridge. There is also the M3 amphibious pontoon bridge and ferry equipment.

Traditionally, armoured and field engineers have been in dedicated brigade close support regiments (21, 22, 23 Air Asslt, 24 Cdo, 26, 32 & 35), with bridging and field support concentrated in the divisional general support regiments (28, 36 & 38). Other principal roles include airfield support (25 & 39 Air Support Regts), geographic support (42 Geographic), and a substantial EOD capability in 33 & 101 Regiments. The RE has five TA regiments – the Royal Monmouthshire Engineers, plus 71, 72, 73 & 75 Regts – and five independent RE squadrons. Additionally, the Regular and TA Works Groups attend to military infrastructure, and the Staff Corps provides civilian engineering, transport and logistics expertise.

The 105mm L118 towed Light Gun. Whether originally equipped with this weapon or not, all close support regiments re-role to the Light Gun for deployment to Afghanistan. This photo shows guns in sand-and-green camouflage, on the establishment of BATU Kenya to support regular and pre-operational training. (Crown Copyright 2011)

A Trojan AVRE operating in Afghanistan. Trojan is based on the Challenger 2 tank chassis; such heavily protected vehicles are able to execute particularly high-risk route clearance tasks in support of ground operations. (Crown Copyright 2010)

Under Army 2020, four Regular regiments (24, 25, 28 & 38) and two Reserve regiments (72 & 73) will disband. Apart from 23 Air Asslt Regt in 16th Air Asslt Bde, all other RE units will be placed in 8th Engineer Bde in the Adaptive Force; this also sees an increase in a number of 'hybrid' units, defined as those containing a mix of Regulars and Reserves. The 8th Engineer Bde will comprise:

25 (Close Support) Engineer Group: 21, 22, 26, 32 & 35 Regts, of which 21 & 32 are hybrid

12 (Force Support) Engineer Group: 36 & 39 Regts; 71 & 75 Reserve Regts; 20 Works Group (Air Support)

170 (Infrastructure Support) Engineer Group: 62, 63, 64 & 66 Works Groups, all hybrid; 65 Reserve Works Group, and Royal Monmouthshire Engineers

29 EOD & Search Group: 33 & 101 Regts, both hybrid. In addition the Group includes 11 EOD Regt, RLC; and 1 Military Working Dogs Regt, RAVC.

ROYAL CORPS OF SIGNALS

While all units contain their own integral signallers responsible for internal communications, all other communications, information systems, electronic warfare and signals intelligence are provided by the Royal Signals (R SIGNALS), now designated the combat command support (CCS) arm. The pre-2013 structure had three brigades (1, 2 & 11) and associated regiments providing CCS to the ARRC and Joint Rapid Reaction Force (JRRF); two close support regiments (1 & 3) as part of the ready divisions; 14 (Electronic Warfare) and 18 (UKSF) Regts, plus five TA regiments (32, 37, 38 (to disband), 39 & 71). Each active brigade also maintained an integral independent signal squadron.

As with the similar corps, Army 2020 places the bulk of the Royal Signals in Force Troops Command, with only 18 Regt retaining its current affiliation. There will be two brigades – the all-Regular 1st Signal Bde supporting the ARRC and JRRF (22 & 30 Regts, and the ARRC Support Bn), and the remainder in 11th Signal Brigade. 14 Regt will move to 1st Intelligence & Surveillance Brigade.

THE INFANTRY

The infantry is not a 'corps', but comprises five regiments of Foot Guards and the regiments of the infantry of the line. Prior to Options 1990, 38 regiments of Guards and line infantry provided a total of 85 Regular and Territorial battalions. In addition, the Special Air Service Regt had three battalions, there were four battalions of Gurkhas, and the Ulster Defence Regt found nine battalions. This gave a total of 101 infantry battalions of all types, plus eight training depots countrywide, and two infantry training schools (at Warminster and Brecon). Considerable change in the intervening years has seen the numbers reduce to 55 battalions of all types in 20 regiments; by 2015 the number of battalions will reduce further to 50.

Pre-Options 1990 there existed three main types of battalion: mechanized (in the tracked FV432 armoured personnel carrier), airportable, and airborne. The Warrior infantry fighting vehicle, which arrived in the late 1980s, provided for true armoured infantry; mechanized infantry was re-categorized into mechanized (tracked), still in FV432, and mechanized (wheeled) in the Saxon APC. There continued to be a large number of battalions in the light role (a category that must not be confused with the regiment then called the Light Infantry).

Army 2020 retains six battalions of armoured infantry in upgraded Warrior IFVs, as well as light infantry, but a number of units will be reclassified as either 'heavy protected mobility' (one battalion in each armoured infantry brigade, equipped with Mastiff), or 'light protected mobility' (one battalion in each infantry brigade, equipped with Foxhound).

The listings on pages 30-39 include all organizational changes since Options 1990. Most significant are the very major changes introduced under FAS 2004 and the accompanying Future Infantry Structure (FIS), which saw the arrival of the 'large/large' regiment. All of the few remaining county regiments were absorbed into the new larger regiments; these continue to be organized on either a national, regional or functional basis, and differ in numbers of battalions.

The infantry also continues to be organized for administrative purposes along divisional lines but, as explained above, these 'divisions' of infantry have no operational function. The original administrative divisions were set up in 1968 when the post-World War II brigade system was finally abandoned. The divisional system organizes the infantry regiments into a number of regionally-based and nationally-based structures; this never included the Parachute Regt, and, while the Gurkhas were then in a division of sorts, it was called a brigade. Small divisional headquarters are to be maintained for the foreseeable future within Headquarters Infantry at Warminster, and all infantry regiments also maintain their own regimental headquarters across the country.

Territorials

Since 1988 there have been four major reorganizations of the Territorial infantry. The complete restructuring of the TA in 1967 had included the creation of some entirely new regional regiments. All of the regiments of the Queen's and Light Divisions had had their Territorial infantry incorporated within their respective large-regiment structures on formation of the latter; but there were also isolated examples, such as the creation of a 3rd (Volunteer) Bn of the Worcestershire & Sherwood Foresters Regt on that regiment's formation in 1971. In 1988 the Yorkshire Volunteers, Wessex Regt and Mercian Volunteers, all created in 1967, were stood down, and in their place a number of 'county' Territorial battalions were re-established within remaining county regiments. The next round of cuts to affect the TA were enacted in 1999. The result was 15 largely regional regiments, each with a single battalion, and linked in a complicated web to the regular infantry regiments. These 15 TA regiments are listed in **Table 7** below.

* * *

The infantry of 2013, where they have come from, and the future effects of Army 2020, are listed below by **administrative divisions**. A summary of the

Table 7: Territorial Infantry Regiments, 1999–2007

3rd (Volunteer) Bn Princess of Wales's Royal Regt	East of England Regt Rifle Volunteers
Royal Rifle Volunteers	East & West Riding Regt
London Regt	Royal Welsh Regt
Lancastrian & Cumbrian Volunteers	Royal Irish Rangers
Tyne-Tees Regt	52nd Lowland Regt
West Midlands Regt	51st Highland Regt
King's & Cheshire Regt	4th (Volunteer) Bn Parachute Regt

Regular and Territorial infantry battalions is shown in regimental order of precedence as **Table 8** (page 32). Except for 4 PARA, the Territorial (or 'Volunteer') infantry battalions are all in the light role, and under Army 2020 they become Reserve light infantry in the brigades of the Adaptable Force.

Guards Division

The five regiments of Foot Guards have been maintained throughout all of the post-World War II reorganizations. However, though all five cap badges are intact, in 1992 the three senior regiments – the Grenadier, Coldstream and Scots Guards – all lost their second battalions. These are officially in 'suspended animation', with a company from each maintained within London District for purely ceremonial functions, thus: No. 2 (Nijmegen) Coy, 2 GREN GDS; No. 7 Coy, 2 COLDM GDS; and F Coy, 2 SG. Therefore, all five Guards regiments now have just one operational battalion. It is normal for two of them to be assigned at any one time to public duties within the Royal Household, all of the battalions rotating between this and conventional infantry roles. Army 2020 will concentrate all five battalions in the London and Home Counties area.

The Guards have never had Territorial battalions, but Options 1990 recreated the London Regt in August 1993, and this was later affiliated to the Guards Division. The LONDONS were to some extent a resurrection of the pre-1938 regiment drawn from London's existing Territorials, but organized along unique lines. The four rifle companies wore different cap badges according to their differing designations: A (London Scottish) Coy, from 1st Bn 51st Highland Regt; B (Queen's Regt) Coy, and C (City of London Fusiliers) Coy, both from 8th Bn Queen's Fusiliers; and D (London Irish Rifles) Coy, from 4th Bn Royal Irish Rangers. In 1999, two companies from 4th (Volunteer) Bn Royal Green Jackets were moved into the London Regt, but were extracted again in 2007 on the formation of The Rifles.

Queen's Division

From its foundation in 1968 the Queen's Division brought together all the old county regiments of London, the Home Counties and eastern England, and the Fusilier regiments, to create three 'large' regiments: the Queen's Regt, the Royal Regt of Fusiliers, and the Royal Anglian Regiment. From an original four Regular battalions each, all three regiments were reduced in two stages; the last of these, following Options 1990, brought them each down to two Regular battalions.

D

TEMPERATE COMBAT DRESS

These three figures all show variations of the Combat 95 dress in temperate 'Woodland' DPM, and PLCE, the latter introduced with SA80 small arms in the 1980s.

1: Guardsman, 1st Battalion Irish Guards; Poland, 2001
This Guardsman on an 'Ulan Eagle' exercise in Poland wears typical issued combat smock, trousers, Norwegian shirt and Mk 6 helmet. He carries the L86A1 LSW, and as an armoured infantry 'dismount' he has an issued chest rig (**1a**), more convenient than standard belt and pouches when riding in an armoured vehicle. Note the blue-red-blue Household Division flash on his right sleeve (**1b**).

2: Sergeant, Queen's Royal Hussars; Germany, c.2002
This NCO on a live-firing range is typical of all tank crews. His armoured crewman's coveralls are worn for training only, a

restriction later applied to his Crewguard helmet. He carries a standard 9mm Browning pistol in its PLCE shoulder harness. To help keep out the cold he has a cotton *shemagh* around his neck (commonly seen after Operation 'Granby' in the Gulf), and stockman's leather gloves purchased while on exercise in Canada.

3: Corporal, 1st Battalion Royal Highland Fusiliers; Northern Ireland, 2002
This soldier is equipped for riot control as part of the Province Reserve Battalion in support of the police in Northern Ireland, and his Mk 6 helmet here has its visor and neck protector attached. Note regimental Mackenzie tartan Tactical Recognition Flash (TRF) on his right sleeve (**3a**). He holds a riot baton and a 1.2-metre Perspex Armadillo shield, while his rifle is slung on his back.

Table 8: Regular & Territorial (Volunteer) Infantry Battalions, 2013

Notes: Regular battalion titles are followed by the official abbreviation (in brackets – note that these are inconsistent), and current role; for all units, these are followed by known Army 2020 roles and brigade assignments (in brackets).

Note that under Army 2020, six battalions will rotate through the Cyprus Garrison in two groups: 2 PWRR/ 1 R ANGLIAN/ 2 R ANGLIAN, and 1 LANCS/ 2 LANCS/ 2 YORKS.

Key to roles: AB = airborne; AI = armoured infantry; AS = air assault; HPM = heavy protected mobility; LPM = light protected mobility; LT = light role; Mech = mechanized; PD = public duties. 'Removed' = battalion ceases to exist due to planned merger.

1st Bn Grenadier Guards (1 GREN GDS); LT/PD; (LT, 11th Bde)

1st Bn Coldstream Guards (1 COLDM GDS); LT; (LT/ PD, London District)

1st Bn Scots Guards (1 SG); AI; (HPM, 12th AI Bde)

1st Bn Irish Guards (1 IG); LT/PD; (LT/PD, London District)

1st Bn Welsh Guards (1 WG); LT; (LPM, 11th Bde)

1st Bn Royal Regt of Scotland (1 SCOTS); LT; (LT, 38th Bde)

2nd Bn Royal Regt of Scotland (2 SCOTS); LT; (LT, 51st Bde)

3rd Bn Royal Regt of Scotland (3 SCOTS); LT; (LPM, 51st Bde)

4th Bn Royal Regt of Scotland (4 SCOTS); LT; (HPM, 20th AI Bde)

5th Bn Royal Regt of Scotland (5 SCOTS); AS; (reduced to Balaklava Coy; LT/PD, 51st Bde)

52nd Lowland Volunteers, 6th Bn Royal Regt of Scotland (52 LOWLAND (V)); (LT, 51st Bde)

51st Highland Volunteers, 7th Bn Royal Regt of Scotland (51 HIGHLAND (V)); (LT, 51st Bde)

1st Bn Princess of Wales's Royal Regt (1 PWRR); AI; (AI, 20th AI Bde)

2nd Bn Princess of Wales's Royal Regt (2 PWRR); LT; (LT, Cyprus Garrison)

3rd Volunteer Bn Princess of Wales's Royal Regt (3 PWRR (V)); (LT, 7th Bde)

1st Bn Duke of Lancaster's Regt (1 LANCS); Mech; (LT, Cyprus Garrison)

2nd Bn Duke of Lancaster's Regt (2 LANCS); LT; (LT, 42nd Bde)

4th Volunteer Bn Duke of Lancaster's Regt (4 LANCS (V)); (LT, 42nd Bde)

1st Bn Royal Regt of Fusiliers (1 RRF); AI; (merges with 2 RRF; AI, 1st AI Bde)

2nd Bn Royal Regt of Fusiliers (2 RRF); LT; (see 1 RRF – removed)

5th Volunteer Bn Royal Regt of Fusiliers (5 RRF(V)); (LT, 51st Bde)

1st Bn Royal Anglian Regt (1 R ANGLIAN); LT; (LT, 7th Bde)

2nd Bn Royal Anglian Regt (2 R ANGLIAN); LT; (LPM, 7th Bde)

3rd Volunteer Bn Royal Anglian Regt (3 R ANGLIAN (V)); (LT, 7th Bde)

1st Bn Yorkshire Regt (1 YORKS); LT; (merges with 2 & 3 YORKS; AI, 12th AI Bde)

2nd Bn Yorkshire Regt (2 YORKS); LT; (see 1 YORKS; LPM, 4th Bde)

3rd Bn Yorkshire Regt (3 YORKS); AI; (see 1 YORKS – removed)

4th Volunteer Bn Yorkshire Regt (4 YORKS (V)); (LT, 4th Bde)

1st Bn Mercian Regt (1 MERCIAN); LT; (merges with 2 & 3 MERCIAN; AI, 1st AI Bde)

2nd Bn Mercian Regt (2 MERCIAN); LT; (merges with 1 & 3 MERCIAN; LT, 42nd Bde)

3rd Bn Mercian Regt (3 MERCIAN); AI; (see 1 & 2 MERCIAN – removed)

4th Volunteer Bn Mercian Regt (4 MERCIAN (V)); (LT, 42nd Bde)

1st Bn Royal Welsh Regt (1 R WELSH); LT; (merges with 2 R WELSH; AI, 12th AI Bde)

2nd Bn Royal Welsh Regt (2 R WELSH); AI; (see 1 R WELSH – removed)

3rd Volunteer Bn Royal Welsh Regt (3 R WELSH (V)); (LT, 11th Bde)

1st Bn Royal Irish Regt (1 R IRISH); AS; (LPM, 7th Bde)

2nd Volunteer Bn Royal Irish Regt (2 R IRISH (V)); (LT, 7th Bde)

1st Bn Rifles (1 RIFLES); LT; (LT, 160th Bde)

2nd Bn Rifles (2 RIFLES); LT; (LT, 38th Bde)

3rd Bn Rifles (3 RIFLES); LT; (LPM, 51st Bde)

4th Bn Rifles (4 RIFLES); Mech; (HPM, 1st AI Bde)

5th Bn Rifles (5 RIFLES); AI; (AI, 20th AI Bde)

6th Volunteer Bn Rifles (6 RIFLES (V)); (LT, 160th Bde)

7th Volunteer Bn Rifles (7 RIFLES (V)); (LT, 38th Bde)

1st Bn Royal Gurkha Rifles (1 RGR); AS; (LT, 11th Bde)

2nd Bn Royal Gurkha Rifles (2 RGR); LT; (LT, Brunei Garrison)

1st Bn Parachute Regt (1 PARA); UKSF

2nd Bn Parachute Regt (2 PARA); AB; (AB, 16th Air Asslt Bde)

3rd Bn Parachute Regt (3 PARA); AB; (AB, 16th Air Asslt Bde)

4th Volunteer Bn Parachute Regt (4 PARA (V)); (LT, 16th Air Asslt Bde)

Royal Gibraltar Regt (RG); LT; (LT, Gibraltar Garrison)

London Regt (LONDONS); (LT, 11th Bde)

One regiment – QUEENS – also absorbed a regiment from outside the Queen's Division; and a further cut in 2015 will reduce RRF to one Regular battalion.

The Princess of Wales's Royal Regt, known as the Tigers, was created in 1992 from the three Regular battalions of the Queen's Regt and the single Regular battalion of the Royal Hampshire Regt (the latter from the Prince of Wales's Division), all merged into two Regular battalions.

The Territorials associated with PWRR have a particularly complicated history. In 1988 elements of 5 QUEENS were amalgamated with elements of 6 RRF to create 8th Bn Queen's Fusiliers. In 1992 this battalion absorbed a company each of the London Scottish and London Irish; and in 1993 all became part of the London Regt, as noted above. The Queen's Regt retained their own cap-badged Territorials as their 5th and 6th/7th Bns, but these were amalgamated in 1999 to become 3 PWRR. At the same time elements of the 6th/7th were amalgamated with 2nd Bn Royal Gloucestershire, Berkshire & Wiltshire Regt, and 5th Bn Royal Green Jackets, to form the Royal Rifle Volunteers. That battalion was retitled 7 RIFLES on the formation of The Rifles in February 2007. Hampshire's Territorials had been part of the Wessex Regt since 1971; in 1994 its two battalions were amalgamated into 2 RGBW, whose subsequent fate has just been mentioned.

In 1992 the Royal Regt of Fusiliers reduced from three Regular battalions (1st, 2nd & 3rd) to two, and from two Territorial battalions (5th & 6th) to one (6th). The RRF then lost the 6th Bn in 1999, when elements became part of the new Tyne-Tees Regiment. However, in April 2006 5th Bn RRF was recreated out of the Royal Fusilier and Light Infantry companies of the Tyne-Tees Regt, also absorbing the Light Infantry company of the East & West Riding Regt (this C (Durham Light Infantry) Coy was transferred to The Rifles in February 2007). 5 RRF is headquartered in North-East England, but maintains embedded companies (often referred to as 'cuckoo' companies) in Birmingham (within 4th Bn Mercian Regt), London (within the London Regt), and Bury (one platoon in 4th Bn Duke of Lancaster's Regiment). As noted, Army 2020 sees the disbandment of 2 RRF by 2015 as its station in Celle, Germany, closes.

Representing the infantry from East Anglia and eastern central England, the Royal Anglian Regt reduced from three Regular battalions (1st, 2nd & 3rd) and three Territorial battalions (5th, 6th & 7th) to two of each category following Options 1990. In 1999 the two remaining Territorial battalions – 6th & 7th – were amalgamated with 3rd Bn Worcestershire & Sherwood Foresters Regt to create the East of England Regiment. In April 2006 this became 3 R ANGLIAN.

King's Division

The English northern county regiments and the Northern Irish regiments originally constituted the King's Division. (Northern Ireland's regiments are dealt with below, as they were taken out of the Division in 1992.) Before Options 1990 the King's Division had eight regiments. One – the Yorkshire Volunteers – was an entirely Territorial regiment with three battalions. The Northern Irish were represented by the Royal Irish Rangers, with two Regular and two Territorial battalions. The remaining six English regiments represented Cumbria (King's Own Royal Border); Merseyside (King's); Yorkshire (Prince of Wales's Own, Green Howards, and Duke of Wellington's); and Lancashire (Queen's Lancashire). These regiments each had one Regular battalion, and all survived Options intact.

The Territorials of the English regiments other than Yorkshire remained as they were pre-Options, thus: 4th Bn KORBR, 5th/8th Bn King's, and 4th & 5th/8th Bns QLR. In 1993 Yorkshire's Territorials were realigned, with 1st, 2nd & 3rd/4th Bns Yorkshire Volunteers becoming, respectively, 4th/5th Bn Green Howards, 3rd Bn PWO, and 3rd Bn DWR.

The 1999 cutbacks to the TA broke up these short-lived battalions. 4/5 GREEN HOWARDS were merged with the Fusilier and Light Infantry Territorials of the north-east to create the Tyne-Tees Regiment; 3 PWO and 3 DWR were merged together with the King's Own Yorkshire Yeomanry to create the East & West Riding Regiment; 4 KORBR and the two Territorial battalions of the QLR became the Lancastrian & Cumbrian Volunteers; and 5/8 KINGS merged with Cheshire's Territorials (from the Mercian Volunteers) into the King's & Cheshire Regiment.

FAS 2004 had a dramatic effect on the regiments of the King's Division, creating two large regiments out of the six: one west of the Pennines – the Duke of Lancaster's Regt, and one east – the Yorkshire Regiment.

The Duke of Lancaster's Regt was created in 2005 following a merger of the KORBR, King's and QLR. Its three Regular battalions were merged into two in 2007. The regiment's Territorials were also formed in 2005 from a merger of the Lancastrian & Cumbrian Volunteers and the two King's Regt companies from the King's & Cheshire Regiment.

The Yorkshire Regt was created in 2006 by a merger of the PWO, Green Howards and DWR. In effect, the resulting three Regular battalions simply retitled themselves under their new cap badge. The regiment has a single battalion of Territorials drawn from the disbanded East & West Riding Regt (bringing one company of PWO and two companies of DWR) and Tyne-Tees Regt (one company of Green Howards). Army 2020 will reduce the three Regular battalions to two.

Prince of Wales's Division

Pre-Options 1990 the Division, a grouping of the regiments of the north and west Midlands, the West Country and Wales, had consisted of nine county regiments each with a single Regular battalion, plus eight Territorial battalions. Following Options, three of the regiments were taken out of the line in two different ways. The Royal Hampshire Regt was merged with the Queen's Regt to become the Princess of Wales's Royal Regiment, as already noted; while the Gloucestershire Regt was amalgamated with the Duke of Edinburgh's Royal Regt in 1994 to create the Royal Gloucestershire, Berkshire & Wiltshire Regiment. The other six – Devon & Dorset, Cheshire, Royal Welch Fusiliers, Royal Regt of Wales, Worcestershire & Sherwood Foresters, and Staffordshire – survived for the time being.

FAS 2004 made major changes to the Division's regiments. For the combined fate of the Devonshire & Dorset Regt and the RGBW Regulars, see below under the Light Division. The remaining five regiments, while retaining five Regular battalions, were made into two new regiments – the Mercian Regt and the Royal Welsh Regiment. The Mercian Regt was formed in 2007 as a result of a merger of the Cheshires, Worcestershire & Sherwood Foresters, and Staffords. The resulting three Regular battalions were, like those of Yorkshire, simply retitled and rebadged. With Army 2020 the three Regular battalions will be merged into two.

The Territorials from Cheshire and Staffordshire had been embodied in two battalions of the Mercian Volunteers (1st & 2nd), while those of

Afghanistan, early 2011: a soldier from 2nd Bn Royal Regt of Scotland with an L129A1 sharpshooter rifle. This replaced the old L96 sniper rifle for designated marksmen and sharpshooters, while trained snipers now carry the 8.58mm L115A3 sniper rifle. Note the PRR headset and ESS goggles. For 'Herrick XIII', 2 SCOTS reinforced 16th Air Asslt Bde. (Crown Copyright 2011)

Worcestershire, Nottinghamshire and Derbyshire were in 3rd Bn Worcestershire & Sherwood Foresters. In 1988 the Mercian Volunteers were disbanded and their manpower moved to the new 3 CHESHIRE and 3 STAFFORDS, while the WFR received a 4th Battalion. In April 1998 the West Midlands Regt was created out of four existing Territorial battalions: 5 RRF, 5 LI, 4 WFR & 3 STAFFORDS. As already stated, 3 WFR was subsumed into the East of England Regt, and 3 CHESHIRE amalgamated with 5/8 KINGS to become the King's & Cheshire Regiment. In July 2006 the King's companies were moved to 4th Bn Duke of Lancaster's Regiment. The whole of the West Midlands Regt, the Cheshire companies of the King's & Cheshire Regt, and the Sherwood Forester companies of the East of England Regt then became 4th Bn Mercian Regt in 2007.

The Royal Welsh Regt was formed in 2006 from the Royal Welch Fusiliers and the Royal Regt of Wales. The new regiment had two Regular battalions, and also incorporated a Territorial battalion which was already called the Royal Welsh Regt; this unit had been formed in 1999 upon the amalgamation of 3 RWF and 2 RRW. Army 2020 will see the merger of the two Regular battalions into one by 2015.

The Royal Irish Regt was created in 1992 and at that time constituted the largest infantry regiment in the Army. It was formed on the amalgamation of the Regulars and Territorials of the Royal Irish Rangers, plus the Northern Ireland Home Service battalions of the Ulster Defence Regiment. The Royal Irish Rangers had been part of the King's Division, but the new regiment was taken out of the Division on account of its size. On its formation it had no fewer than 11 battalions in three classes: two Regular battalions (1st & 2nd); seven Home Service battalions (all former UDR battalions); and two TA battalions (4th & 5th), the latter retaining the title of Royal Irish Rangers.

Within a year of formation the two Regular battalions had been amalgamated, and in 2001, with the calming of the Troubles in Northern Ireland, the Home Service battalions were reduced to three. With the end of Operation 'Banner' in Northern Ireland the Home Service battalions were finally disbanded in July 2007, and the one remaining Territorial battalion lost its Ranger title (although all soldiers, Regulars and Territorials, continue to be called 'Rangers'). In 2013 the Royal Irish Regt comprised just one Regular and one Territorial battalion, and was moved into the Prince of Wales's Division.

Light Division

The most imaginative reorganization to come out of FIS 2004 was the transformation in 2007 of the regiments of the Light Division into a single 'large/large regiment' called The Rifles. The original regiments of the Light Division – the Light Infantry and the Royal Green Jackets – were two 'large' regiments created in 1968 and 1966 respectively, which had originally comprised six Regular battalions (three each for both regiments) and two (later six) Territorial battalions (four LI and two RGJ). Options 1990 saw each regiment reduced to two Regular battalions in 1992.

When faced with the impact of FIS 2004, the LI and RGJ recognized that there was great sense in creating a much larger regiment. They were joined by the Devon & Dorsets and the RGBW, both from the Prince of Wales's Division and now amalgamated into one battalion. These latter two regiments went through a strange transitional period of being called 'Light Infantry' (e.g. the D & D Light Infantry) and wearing the green beret of the Light Division before the actual formation of The Rifles. The five Regular battalions of The Rifles were derived thus: 1 RIFLES from the D & D and RGBW LI; 2 RIFLES from 1 RGJ; 3 RIFLES from 2 LI; 4 RIFLES from 2 RGJ; and 5 RIFLES from 1 LI.

The story of the RGJ Territorials – 4 RGJ & 5 RGJ – is described above under the PWRR and the London Regiment. The four battalions of LI Territorials transitioned in 1999: elements of 5 LI became part of the West Midlands Regt; 6 LI became part of the Royal Rifle Volunteers; 7 LI became part of the Tyne-Tees Regt; and 8 LI, the remnants of which had become part of the King's Own Yorkshire Yeomanry in 1987, subsequently became part of the East & West Riding Regiment. The new Rifles also took back all of their Territorials to create two 'new' Territorial battalions: 6 RIFLES from the Rifle Volunteers, and 7 RIFLES from the Royal Rifle Volunteers and the two RGJ companies from the London Regiment.

Scottish Division

Pre-Options 1990 this had seven Regular regiments, but in 1994 the Queen's Own Highlanders were amalgamated with the Gordon Highlanders to create The Highlanders. Scotland's Territorials had been organized in two regiments: the 52nd Lowland Volunteers (two battalions), and the 51st Highland Volunteers

OPERATIONS & TRAINING OVERSEAS

1: Rifleman, 2nd Battalion Royal Gurkha Rifles; Sierra Leone, 2003

Operations begun in Sierra Leone in 2000 subsequently evolved into training tasks, and this soldier is shown during a tactics demonstration to the Sierra Leone Army in 2003. His shirt and trousers, while very similar to Combat 95s, are the lighter-weight Tropical Combats. He wears standard PLCE and carries the recently upgraded L85A2 rifle, but here he wields a *kukri*, with which all Gurkhas are also armed.

2: Warrant Officer, 1st Battalion Royal Green Jackets; Kosovo, 2005

The UK also continued to be engaged in Kosovo as late as 2005, when 1 RGJ was deployed there on peacekeeping duties. This company sergeant major wears a privately-purchased windproof smock in Woodland DPM. Regimental identification is shown in the Rifle-green beret, the cap badge (**2a**), and the rank slide on the chest strap with a small bugle-horn-and-'RGJ' badge below his crown rank badge. Note too the small Union flag on the left shoulder; this national emblem was by this date universally worn on Combat Dress. He also wears a Vest, Tactical, Load-Carrying, often issued in place of PLCE for operational deployments.

3: Corporal, Royal Signals; Kenya, 2009

Something of a revolution in collective training took place from the mid-1990s with the introduction of laser Tactical Engagement Simulation (TES), allowing for realistic force-on-force exercises. This Royal Signals NCO training in Kenya wears a helmet band and 'vest' with TES sensors over his PLCE and Enhanced Combat Body Armour (ECBA); note too the laser transmitter behind the yellow-painted blank-firing attachment on his rifle. The ECBA may appear incongruous in this context, but body armour became mandatory for training. Note the rank slide worn on the strap offset on its plate pocket (**3a**), but hidden here by the TES 'vest'.

3

2

1

3a

ROYAL
SIGNALS

2a

(three battalions) – the anachronistic use of these numbers commemorating the two Scottish divisions of World War II. In 1995, 1st Bn 52nd Lowland became 3rd Bn Royal Highland Fusiliers, and 2nd Bn 52nd Lowland became simply the Lowland Volunteers. Also in 1995, while 1st Bn 51st Highland Volunteers retained its title, 2nd Bn 51st Highland became 7th/8th Bn Argyll and Sutherland Highlanders, and 3rd Bn 51st Highland became 3rd Bn The Highlanders. 1999 saw them all reduced to two single-battalion Territorial regiments, the two battalions of lowlanders becoming the 52nd Lowland Regt and the three battalions of highlanders the 51st Highland Regiment.

In 2006, FIS established a single 'large/large' infantry regiment of five Regular and two Territorial battalions for Scotland – the Royal Regiment of Scotland. For largely political reasons the antecedent titles were retained within the single regiment: The Royal Scots Borderers, 1st Bn SCOTS (formed from an amalgamation of the Royal Scots and the King's Own Scottish Borderers); The Royal Highland Fusiliers, 2nd Bn SCOTS; The Black Watch, 3rd Bn SCOTS; The Highlanders, 4th Bn SCOTS; and The Argyllshire and Sutherland Highlanders, 5th Bn SCOTS. This 5 SCOTS was reduced in 2013 to a single company (Balaklava Coy) confined to a purely ceremonial role in Scotland. The two TA battalions are 52nd Lowland, 6 SCOTS; and 51st Highland, 7 SCOTS.

*   *   *

The following infantry units are separate from the administrative divisional organization:

Parachute Regiment

The Paras were never incorporated in the divisional structure, and have been largely unaffected by any of the amalgamations and disbandments of units since World War II; indeed, the three Regular battalions that survived the immediate post-war reductions (1st, 2nd & 3rd) survive to this day. In 1993, following Options, the three Territorial battalions (4th, 10th & 15th) were reduced to just one, 4 PARA.

It has been Army policy to maintain a minimum of two Regular battalions trained in the parachute role; this has generally been rotated through the three, with the out-of-role battalion being held as a normal light-role infantry battalion (although in the 1970s one battalion converted to the mechanized role). The parachute-role battalions are assigned to their own specialist formation, 16th Air Asslt Brigade. However, as a result of FAS 2004, in 2006 the 1st Bn was permanently assigned to the new Special Forces Support Group within the Directorate of Special Forces.

Royal Gurkha Rifles

Prior to Options 1990 there were four regiments of Gurkha Rifles: 2nd King Edward VII's Own, 6th Queen Elizabeth's Own, 7th Duke of Edinburgh's Own, and 10th Princess Mary's Own. Each had a single battalion (2nd Bn 7th Gurkhas having been disbanded in 1987). Options created the Royal Gurkha Rifles in 1994, originally with three battalions but reduced to two in 1996. Up until that date the Gurkhas always formed a major part of the Hong Kong and Brunei garrisons, and they still maintain one

The Parachute Regt has jealously guarded its parachuting skills ever since its formation. Today the likelihood of a complete unit conducting a parachute assault is very small, but maintaining the skill gives the Paras an important hardened edge and additional *esprit de corps*. Here soldiers from 3 PARA practice on Salisbury Plain in 2012 for their Airborne Task Force role. (Crown Copyright 2012)

Afghanistan, 2010: an 81mm mortar team firing from a forward operating base engages insurgents during 'Herrick XII'. This team came from the Gurkha Reinforcement Company attached to 1st Bn Mercian Regt for a two-year period to help alleviate manpower shortages. The formation patch visible on the right-hand Gurkha's left sleeve is the black rat of 4th Mech Bde, with the Afghan national patch beside it, both below a small Union flag. (Crown Copyright 2010)

battalion in Brunei, largely funded by the Sultan.

For administration purposes the RGR is grouped with Gurkha Signals, Engineers and Logistics in the Brigade of Gurkhas. There are also two additional infantry companies permanently assigned as demonstration troops: Sittang Coy to RMA Sandhurst, and Mandalay Coy to the Infantry Battle School, Brecon. It should be noted too that to alleviate infantry undermanning elsewhere three complete Gurkha companies, known as reinforcement companies, were maintained within three British battalions up until 2014.

Royal Gibraltar Regiment

Originally a Reserve unit, the Royal Gibraltar Regt was placed on the Regular establishment following the withdrawal of the British Army garrison from Gibraltar in 1991. It comprises two Regular and one Reserve companies plus an artillery troop.

United Kingdom Special Forces

In 1987 the special forces were brought together in UKSF, a new organization established to better coordinate SF activities. The requirement for additional forces led in 2005 to the creation of the Special Reconnaissance Regt (SRR), the nucleus for which was provided by 14 Intelligence Company, a unit previously focused on the intelligence campaign in Northern Ireland. In 2005 the Special Forces Support Group was also created out of a number of existing units to provide additional direct support to UKSF. The organization of UKSF is:

22 Special Air Service Regt

Special Boat Service (Royal Marines)

Special Reconnaissance Regt

21 Special Air Service Regt (Reserve)

23 Special Air Service Regt (Volunteers)

Special Forces Support Group: 1 PARA, F Coy Royal Marines, 18 Signal Regt, Joint SF Aviation Wing

Apache Longbows at Camp Bastion airfield in Afghanistan, 2011. Procured originally to combat Group of Soviet Forces Germany in the anti-armour role, the Apache has provided critical air cover for ground forces during counter-insurgency operations in Iraq and Afghanistan. It equips two attack regiments of the Army Air Corps. (Crown Copyright 2011)

Army Air Corps

The AAC provides the Army's own aviation support in peace and war. In peacetime the majority of AAC units are under the Joint Helicopter Command, and due to the joint nature of most operations the AAC is invariably joined by helicopters of the RN or RAF. The latter's helicopters, with their heavier lift capability, have a particularly important role in support of ground operations. The AAC also includes significant numbers of integrated RLC, REME and AGC personnel.

For many years Army aviation had a largely support function, but since their earliest days helicopters were armed to provide fire support on the battlefield. The most successful of these was the Lynx TOW, but the introduction of the Apache attack helicopter, delivery of which was completed in 2007, has provided the AAC with a true combat capability. The AAC today fulfils five roles: offensive action in support of the land battle; intelligence, surveillance, target acquisition and reconnaissance (ISTAR); artillery fire control; command support; and general utility through the carriage of personnel and equipment and casualty evacuation.

To support these roles the AAC employs six types of helicopter and one type of fixed-wing aircraft: Attack Helicopter (AH) Mk 1 – the Westland Apache; Westland Lynx AH 7, AH 9 and AH 9A (to be replaced from 2014 with 'Future Lynx', to be known as Wildcat AH 1); Westland Gazelle AH 1; Eurocopter AS350BB Squirrel HT 2 (for training only); Bell 212 AH 2 (in an independent flight in Brunei only); Eurocopter AS365N3 Dauphin II (supporting UKSF); and the fixed-wing Britten-Norman Islander AL 1/CC 2 and Defender AL 1/AL 2.

In 2013 the AAC had two Apache attack regiments (3 & 4 AAC); two Lynx regiments (1 & 9 AAC); one Gazelle regiment (5 AAC); two training regiments (2 & 7 AAC); and one Territorial regiment (6 AAC). By 2016, 1 AAC and 9 AAC will merge and be re-equipped with Wildcat. The AAC also maintains four independent squadrons and four independent flights, including a jungle training flight in Brunei and a training flight at BATUS in Canada.

Royal Army Chaplains' Department

The Royal Army Chaplains' Department (RAChD) provides ordained clergy to the Army. The chaplains, known as 'padres', are predominantly Christian but the Department also includes Jewish chaplains. In recent times the Army has also made provision for other faiths, although their inclusion in the RAChD is not formal.

Royal Logistic Corps

On its formation in 1992 the RLC represented a major organizational change by bringing together the Army's main transport and supply organizations. It was formed from an amalgamation of the Royal Corps of Transport, Royal Army Ordnance Corps, Royal Pioneer Corps, Army Catering Corps, and the postal and courier elements of the RE (who retain their RE cap badge). The RLC contains more regiments and units than any other arm or service.

The Corps is primarily responsible for the storage and delivery of all combat supplies (fuel, rations, water and ammunition), as well as some specialist enabling activities including EOD (shared with the RE) and movement. Pre-Army 2020 there have been four main functional areas: Formation Support (1, 2, 3, 4 & 12 Logistic Support Regts); Force Support (6, 7, 9 & 27 Logistic Regts, and 10 Queen's Own Gurkha Logistic Regt); Enabling (11 EOD, 17 Port & Maritime, 23 Pioneer, 24 (Postal & Courier), & 29 (Transport & Movement) Regts; and Training (5 & 25 Regiments). Apart from 11 EOD Regt, which is placed in 29 EOD & Search Group in 8th Engineer Bde, and 13 Air Asslt Support Regt in 16th Air Asslt Bde, Army 2020 reduces and reclassifies units and places them in three logistic brigades:

101st Logistic Brigade: 1, 3 & 4 Close Support Logistic Regts; 9, 10 (Gurkha) & 27 Theatre Logistic Regts; 151, 154 & 157 Reserve Transport Regts; 156 Reserve Supply Regiment

102nd Logistic Brigade: 6 & 7 Force Logistic Regts; 150 & 158 Reserve Transport Regts; 159 Reserve Supply Regiment

104th Logistic Brigade: 17 Port & Maritime Regt; 165 Reserve Port & Enabling Regt; 29 & 162 Reserve Postal, Courier & Movement Regts; 152 Reserve Fuel Support Regt; 167 Reserve Catering Support Regt; 2 Operational Support Group.

Army Medical Services

The Army Medical Services (AMS) were established to administer the four corps providing medical and health care for the Army: the Royal Army Medical Corps (RAMC), Royal Army Veterinary Corps (RAVC), Royal Army Dental Corps (RADC), and Queen Alexandra's Royal Army Nursing Corps (QARANC). Reservists are of critical importance to the AMS, and include the First Aid Nursing Yeomanry (Princess Royal's Volunteer Corps). The RAVC, headquartered at Melton Mowbray, is responsible for the provision, training and care of animals (mainly horses and dogs, but including some more exotic regimental mascots). It includes the 1st Military Working Dog Regt, whose 101st–105th MWD Sqns are distributed throughout the Army.

In general terms the Regular and TA medical regiments have provided direct support to the Field Army, with 2nd Medical Bde containing all the Field Hospitals. Under the Army 2020 rationalization, 101st Logistic Bde will have 1, 4 & 5 Armd Medical Regts; 102nd Logistic Bde will have 2 & 3 Medical Regts (both hybrid) and three Reserve Medical Regts; and 16 Medical Regt, another hybrid, is allotted to 16th Air Asslt Brigade. 2nd Medical Bde will contain the three Regular Field Hospitals (22, 33 & 34), ten Reserve Field Hospitals, and three Reserve Support units.

Corps of Royal Electrical and Mechanical Engineers

REME consists entirely of technicians and mechanics responsible for equipment support: the repair and maintenance and, where necessary, recovery of all equipment. Corps personnel are deployed in every unit, invariably grouped in Light Aid Detachments (LADs), but belong to a number of parent REME battalions. The five Close Support Battalions (1, 2, 3, 4 & 6), 19 Combat

An Ammunition Technical Officer of the Royal Logistic Corps, protected by a Mk VI Explosive Ordnance Disposal suit, dealing with a suspect IED. These men and women, and their counterparts in the RE, have saved countless military and civilian lives at home as well as overseas. (Photo courtesy Bob Graham)

Service Support Bn (disbanded 2013), and 7 Air Asslt Bn were all assigned to Regular brigades, with two Force Support Battalions (101 & 104) assigned to 102nd and 101st Logistic Brigades respectively. The REME had no formed Territorial battalions, but the future Reserves plan creates four (101, 102, 104 & 106) from disbanded RLC units.

Under Army 2020, 7 Air Asslt Bn REME remains with 16th Air Asslt Bde; all other REME battalions are reclassified and reorganized as follows:
101st Logistic Brigade: 3, 4 & 6 Armd Close Support Bns; 5 Force Support Bn (formed from 101 & 104 Bns); 103 & 105 Reserve Battalions
102nd Logistic Brigade: 1 & 2 Close Support Bns; 101, 102, 104 & 106 Reserve Battalions.

Adjutant General's Corps

The second large corps created out of Options was the AGC, an amalgamation of the administrative services to form four branches. Except for the Provost branch, AGC personnel are individually distributed across the Army. The four AGC branches are:
Provost Branch – comprising the Royal Military Police (RMP), Military Provost Staff (MPS) and Military Provost Guard Service (MPGS). Army 2020 creates the 1st Military Police Bde, a hybrid Regular and Reserve formation which will contain the three RMP regiments (1, 3 & 4), the Special Investigations Branch Regt, a new Special Operations Unit, and the Military Corrective Training Centre.
Army Legal Services (ALS) – incorporating the Army Legal Corps.
Staff and Personnel Services (SPS) – comprising the Royal Army Pay Corps (RAPC), and the clerks of the RAOC and all other regiments and corps.
Educational and Training Services (ETS) – incorporating the Royal Army Educational Corps (RAEC).

The majority of personnel in the AGC wear that Corps' cap badge, but elements of some branches, e.g. the RMP, retain their old badges.

Small Arms School Corps

The SASC, whose headquarters is at Warminster, is responsible for maintaining proficiency across the Army in small arms, support weapons and range management. Barely 160 strong, it comprises only senior NCOs and officers, spread around the Army's schools and main range complexes.

OPERATION 'TELIC', IRAQ

1: Private, 1st Battalion Black Watch; Basrah, April 2003
Uniforms and equipment for the early stages of Operation 'Telic' were little changed from 'Granby' 12 years earlier. This mixture of Woodland and Desert DPM Combats demonstrates the limited availability of desert clothing at that stage. Enhanced CBA, new for this campaign, is characterized by the ballistic plate in the chest pocket. 7th Armd Bde was the only formation to wear its patch on the right arm **(1a)**, and regimental TRFs were still not universal at this date.

2: Lance Corporal, Royal Electrical and Mechanical Engineers, 2006
This REME lance corporal is on convoy escort duties, and his L85A2 rifle with underbarrel grenade launcher demonstrates that CSS soldiers had to be trained and ready to fight like any others. His windproof smock in Desert DPM is largely obscured by Kestrel body armour, introduced in late 2005 for vehicle top-cover sentries. This bulky and uncomfortable 'Elvis suit' was an interim measure before Osprey armour started to be provided from late 2006.

3: Private, 1st Battalion Yorkshire Regiment, 2009
This Fijian soldier wears Osprey Mk 2 armour while on checkpoint duty. The final development of Desert Combats is shown with the Under Body Armour Combat Shirt (UBACS); the upper sleeve pockets have the regimental TRF on the right arm **(see 3a)** and the 20th Armd Bde patch on the left **(see 3b)**. He is heavily laden: a PRR on his chest, a spare ammunition bag for his Minimi LMG at his left hip, and the bulk of his kit in a daysack. Strapped to this is a Camelbak water carrier, and inside the sack electronic countermeasures equipment is identified by its distinctive antenna.

2

3a

3

1

1a

3b

Intelligence Corps

The overall role of the INT CORPS is to collect information and provide intelligence for defence and security requirements. The headquarters is at the Defence Intelligence & Security Centre, Chicksands, and operations in the field have been conducted by the three Regular and two Reserve multi-function battalions.

Army 2020 will see far greater integration of intelligence and surveillance assets in the 1st Intelligence & Surveillance Bde, which will also include RA and R SIGNALS units as noted above. In addition to the Regular Military Intelligence battalions (1, 2 & 4), there will be four Reserve battalions (3, 5, 6 & 7); two hybrid units – the Land Intelligence Fusion Centre, and the Defence Cultural Specialist Unit; and the Specialist Group Military Intelligence, a Reserve unit.

Royal Army Physical Training Corps

The RAPTC, which received its royal title in 2010, is headquartered at Aldershot with the Army School of Physical Training. This small corps of largely non-commissioned officers is responsible for physical training and education, and has personnel deployed in every unit of the Army.

The SA80 family (minus the L98A1 cadet rifle). The SA80 replaced the self-loading rifle, light machine gun and sub-machine gun from 1985, receiving major upgrades to A2 standard in 2000–2002. From top to bottom: L85A2 individual weapon with Sight Unit Small Arms Trilux (SUSAT); L85A2 with 'iron sights'; L86A2 light support weapon (not to scale); and L22A2 carbine. (Crown Copyright)

Corps of Army Music

The CAMUS was established in 1994, and contains all remaining military bands. Its headquarters are at Kneller Hall, co-located with the Royal Military School of Music. Prior to Options there were 69 bands, each regiment and corps having its own; but the great majority were lost or reduced from 1993 onwards, and the figure today stands at 23 Regular and 19 Territorial bands. All regiments of the Household Division have retained their own bands, but each corps now has a single band. The cavalry has been reduced to two bands, one 'heavy' and one 'light', and the infantry now have just one band per division or similar grouping. While providing music is the core function of military bandsmen, on operations they also continue to provide support to the Army Medical Services.

Soldier from 1st Bn Mercian Regt in Afghanistan during 'Herrick XII'. His L85A2 rifle has all the operational modifications for this weapon: 'picatinny rail' handguard, forward handgrip/bipod, LLM01 laser aiming module, and Advanced Combat Optical Sight (ACOG). The Mk 6A helmet has a carrying plate for the Helmet Mounted Night Vision System (HMNVS). Note the 'zap' number and blood group marked on his glove. (Crown Copyright 2010)

British Overseas Territories

In addition, three British Overseas Territories have units considered part of the British Army:

Bermuda Regiment – a battalion-sized light infantry unit made up largely of conscripts.

Falkland Islands Defence Force – a Reserve light infantry company.

Royal Montserrat Defence Force – about 20 Reserve personnel.

Table 9: Small Arms & Support Weapons, 2013

Glock 17 Pistol 9mm; standard issue from 2013, replacing L9A1 Browning and P226 SIG-Sauer.

L85A2 Assault Rifle; L85A2 Light Support Weapon; L22A2 Carbine 5.56mm SA80 standard small arms family; A2 versions of rifle and LSW replaced A1 from 2000. L123A1 40mm Underbarrel Grenade Launcher on L85A2.

L129A1 Sharpshooter Rifle 7.62mm Law Enforcement International LM7; replaced L118A1 (L96) for marksmen and sharpshooters.

L115A3 Sniper Rifle 8.58mm; replaced L118A1 for trained snipers.

M82A1 Anti-Materiel Rifle .50cal (12.7mm) Barrett.

L74A1 Combat Shotgun 12 bore, 8-shot, semi-automatic patrol weapon.

HK53 Carbine 5.56mm; used by RMP close-protection teams and UKSF.

L119A1 Assault Rifle 5.56mm Colt Canada C8; used by 16th Air Asslt Bde Pathfinders and UKSF.

L108A1 & L110A1 Light Machine Gun 5.56mm Minimi; has largely replaced LSW in front-line service. L110A1 is short-barrelled airborne version.

L7A2 General Purpose Machine Gun 7.62mm FN MAG; used in both dismounted (bipod) and sustained-fire (tripod) roles.

L2A1 Heavy Machine Gun .50cal (12.7mm) M2 Browning.

L134A1 Grenade Launcher 40mm Heckler & Koch automatic.

51mm Light Mortar Standard infantry platoon mortar.

60mm Light Mortar Hirtenberger M6-895; UOR replacement for 51mm Light Mortar.

L16 81mm Mortar Medium mortar; used both dismounted and vehicle-mounted.

L72A9 Anti-Structure Weapon Development of 66mm Light Anti-armour Weapon (LAW).

AT4 Anti-tank Weapon Quantities procured for Operation 'Herrick'.

MBT LAW Main Battle Tank Light Anti-armour Weapon; replacing LAW80.

Javelin FGM-148 anti-tank guided weapon system; replaced Milan.

THE ARMY ON OPERATIONS AND AT WAR

Warrior IFV of 1st Bn Princess of Wales's Royal Regt in Afghanistan, 2011. First entering service in 1988, Warrior has proved one of the Army's most successful fighting vehicles; this example shows typical operational modifications including Chobham side armour and bar armour. Warrior will receive a major upgrade programme to equip six armoured infantry battalions in Army 2020. (Crown Copyright 2011)

Command

The British Army does not conduct operations in isolation from the other services; even in Northern Ireland – a predominantly Army operation – the other two armed services were actively involved. All operations also include significant elements from other government agencies, and operations in Northern Ireland were, of course, led by the police for the greater part of the campaign.

Operations of any scale are therefore tri-service or 'joint' operations, and are commanded by a joint force commander who may be provided by the Joint Force Headquarters (JFHQ), which sits within the Permanent Joint Headquarters (PJHQ) established at Northwood, Middlesex, in 1996. PJHQ is commanded by the Chief of Joint Operations (CJO), a tri-service three-star post.

Operations overseas, especially of a medium and large-scale nature, tend also to be part of international coalitions, and these entail the appointment of a British national component commander (who is invariably double-hatted as the joint force commander) in the coalition headquarters. He will exercise direct command of his assigned maritime, land and air components through their respective commanders, and may have direct command of certain national support elements. Operations outside the UK are commanded by the joint force commander working to the CJO at PJHQ. Should occasion arise inside the UK, command is provided by the Standing Joint Commander (SJC). CLF is permanently double-hatted as the SJC, and Headquarters SJC, consisting of personnel drawn from all three services, is co-located with Army HQ.

3

3a

ISAF
کمک او همکاری

1

2

Afghanistan, 2011: Personal Clothing System (Combat Uniform) and integrated load-carrying equipment demonstrated by a soldier from 2nd Bn Royal Regiment of Scotland. MTP was by now almost universal, but he still wears Desert DPM gloves. Just visible ahead of the circular ISAF patch on his sleeve is the regimental TRF, a version of the cap badge (dark yellow lion on black saltire, on olive drab). The HMNVS can be seen clearly on his helmet.

(Crown Copyright 2011)

Ready Forces

In peacetime the Army has always maintained forces at various states of readiness and training. Such plans are invariably subject to major change during the conduct of operations, acknowledging the fact that no plan survives contact with the enemy. This principle will apply just the same for the Army 2020 structures.

In 1996 the Joint Rapid Reaction Force (JRRF) was set up, to make available a rapidly deployable array of forces drawn from all three services to meet demands as they arose. The JRRF is, in effect, CJO's assigned deployable force. The core of the JRRF was 16th Air Asslt Bde and, from the Royal Navy, 3rd Commando Bde, but other operationally-ready formations and units from the Field Army could be assigned as required. To meet this demand the Army maintained one brigade-sized group at 'high readiness'; an airborne task force (a battalion-sized all-arms grouping) at 'very high readiness'; and the Spearhead Lead Element (a further battalion-sized grouping) at 'extremely high readiness'. The JRRF was deployed, for example, on Operation 'Barras' to Sierra Leone in 2000. Since the onset of the war in Iraq and the overlapping and subsequent demands of the war in Afghanistan, high-readiness brigades and units have been routinely assigned to these operations, and have therefore been unavailable to the JRRF.

The principles of organization are the same, whether the requirement is for general (or conventional) war – that is, operations of the type that NATO was trained to fight against the Warsaw Pact on the central front in Europe, and actually fought against Iraq in the two Gulf Wars in 1991 and 2003 – or for all other operations. The generic term for the latter is 'Operations Other Than War' (OOTW). In such operations units might be entirely re-roled (as occurred in Northern Ireland, when artillery and armoured regiments were on occasion re-roled as infantry), or organized to conduct expeditionary operations in a counter-insurgency role.

Tactical formations – divisions and their subordinate brigades – contain combinations of all arms and services, and are termed combined-arms formations. A division will be task-organized to achieve its assigned mission, and, while the division might allocate additional combat support and combat service support units to its brigades, some of these units will also be retained as divisional troops. The brigade level is usually the lowest which can operate in general war independently of a divisional structure, as it has the capacity to control its own combat support and combat service support units, and all operations require considerable logistic and enabling resources. As noted earlier, divisions and brigades have had relatively permanently assigned support units, but Army 2020 places the majority of these in Force Troops Command, available to be assigned as required.

Battlegroups

Brigades will also task-organize and, to achieve the correct balance of forces, will create battlegroups out of their combat units. A battlegroup might, for example, comprise two squadrons of tanks and two companies of infantry, this being referred to as a 'square' battlegroup and shown in task organization tables as '2, 2'. An infantry-heavy battlegroup of, say, one tank squadron and three infantry companies, would be shown as '1, 3'. These battlegroups will usually retain their own 'cap-badged' reconnaissance troops/platoons, but infantry mortars and especially infantry anti-tank sub-units will also be allocated according to brigade requirements. Battlegroups might be allocated some combat support elements, such as a troop or squadron of engineers for specific tasks, but, apart from their forward fire control teams (artillery battery commanders and their assigned forward observation officers, (FOOs)), artillery is usually controlled at the highest level to provide the best possible fire support across the brigade or division.

The battlegroup can also sub-divide if required, by combining armoured squadrons and infantry companies and adding, perhaps, a section of anti-tank weapons, an artillery FOO, a mortar fire controller (MFC) and a troop of engineers. Such all-arms groupings were once called 'combat teams' but are more properly known as 'company/squadron groups'. These groups will most often consist of a full company of infantry and a full squadron of tanks, with a troop of the latter designated as intimate support to the infantry.

For the entirety of the modern army's existence, groupings of the main combat arms – the tanks and the infantry – have been *ad hoc*, and all attempts to create permanent groupings in war and in peace have been defied. An armoured regiment or an infantry battalion will therefore very rarely conduct operations as a complete cap-badged unit. Enduring pressures on manpower also mean that they often receive considerable reinforcements from other cap badges prior to embarking on operations.

OPERATIONS SINCE 1990

The demands of the Cold War and the threat of a Warsaw Pact attack were the main focus of military planning for decades. To that end the Army was organized, equipped and trained primarily for its role in NATO, although this considerable military effort, especially to BAOR, was never classified as 'operational'. The Army was constantly distracted from this focus by actual operations elsewhere, such as Northern Ireland and long-standing commitments to the United Nations. The latter are now greatly reduced, but Operation 'Tosca' has a company group continuing to support the UN on the Green Line in Cyprus.

The years of training for general war bore fruit in 1990–91 in the successful campaign to liberate Kuwait (the First Gulf War) on Operation 'Granby', during which the Army deployed 1st Armd Div with two armoured brigades (4th and 7th) and an array of additional units. However, the 1990s were largely dominated by peacekeeping operations in the former Yugoslavia – in Bosnia and, from 1999, in Kosovo. On Operation 'Grapple', begun in February 1992, the UK contributed a large battlegroup to the UN Protection Force (UNPROFOR) in Bosnia. From late 1995 a NATO Implementation Force (IFOR) relieved UNPROFOR on Operation 'Resolute'; this transformed into Operation 'Lodestar' when IFOR became the Stabilisation Force (SFOR) in December 1996. The British contribution

Land Rover WMIK of the Anti-Tank Platoon, 1st Bn Parachute Regt during the opening stages of Operation 'Telic' in Iraq, March 2003. Note the Milan firing post and GPMG; just left of the standing Para, the 'glint' panels for IFF; the spare Milan anti-tank guided missiles at the rear; and the crew's stowed kit. (Author's photo)

Iraq, March 2003: three officers on the staff of Tactical Headquarters 1st Armd Div with Forward Headquarters 1st US Marine Division. Due to the perceived Iraqi chemical threat they are dressed (or partially so) in bulky CBRN kit in Woodland DPM; the officer at left also has Combat Body Armour, but in Desert DPM. (Author's photo)

Iraq, 2007: an example of the Army's 'legacy' equipment, the FV430 series was first brought into service in the 1960s. Although they were long obsolete as armoured personnel carriers, urgent requirements for heavily-protected patrol vehicles in Iraq led to the introduction of the Mk 3 Bulldog in late 2006. In addition to extra armour and a GPMG turret, this Bulldog of 1st Bn Royal Green Jackets photographed in Basrah has a counter-IED array. (Crown Copyright 2007)

saw HQs 1st Armd Div and 3rd Div act in turn as HQ Multi-National Division South-West. Four brigades – 4th Mech, 1st Mech, 20th Armd & 7th Armd – rotated in that order through Bosnia between October 1995 and late 1997, after which British forces began to be reduced. From 2004 European Union Force (EUFOR) assumed responsibility for peacekeeping, and the UK ceased its permanent commitment to Bosnia in 2007.

The UK contribution to the NATO peacekeeping force in Kosovo (KFOR) began in 1999 with the deployment of 1 R IRISH under Operation 'Agricola'. Initial commitment involved a battalion-sized group, subsequently reduced to a limited permanent force. However, crises saw 1 RGJ deployed as the Spearhead Lead Element in 2005, and a further surge by 2 RIFLES in 2008. The UK's permanent contribution ceased in 2009, except for a small number of staff and specialists.

Elsewhere, 1999 saw elements of 2 RGR and UKSF deploy to East Timor on Operation 'Warden'. The causes of peacekeeping and humanitarian relief then led directly to the UK's intervention in Sierra Leone in 2000–01. Troops were deployed initially to support the UN mission by providing an infantry battalion (2 R ANGLIAN, later 1 R IRISH) to an International Military Assistance and Training Team (IMATT) on Operation 'Palliser', but the civil war required an escalated response under a Joint Task Force based on a reinforced 1 PARA battlegroup. Elements of 1 PARA and 22 SAS were also engaged in Operation 'Barras' to release military hostages captured by local rebels. Other than this, Africa has largely been the province of training teams, but the after-effects of the 'Arab Spring' saw a UKSF involvement in Libya in 2011 on Operation 'Ellamy', and the deployment of advisers and trainers to Mali in 2013.

Throughout the period until 2007 the backdrop of the Troubles in Northern Ireland required the lengthiest operation in British military history: Operation 'Banner'. In the worst days of the early 1970s around 28,000 soldiers were deployed in the Province, but a steady state of around 10,000 was assumed by the mid-1980s. Headquarters Northern Ireland deployed its three brigades with six resident infantry battalions on, originally, 18-month and subsequently two-year tours. Additionally, a minimum of four units, not always infantry, deployed on four-and-a-half-month, later six-month 'roulement' tours, together with a great host of other units. From the turn of the century active operations by soldiers on the ground had greatly diminished, but in total 763 security force personnel were killed, 637 of them British soldiers, before operations ended on 31 July 2007. While there remains an undercurrent of extremist activity, and two Royal Engineers were murdered in 2009, the situation is now 'normalized'. The Army is no longer responsible for security in the Province,

'Herrick XVII', Afghanistan, 2013: an infantryman from 4th Mech Bde firing during a contact. He wears Osprey Mk 4 armour, and pelvic ('plum') protection. In 2011, three tiers of this protection were introduced; when 'outside the wire' soldiers must wear Tier 1 'combat knickers' as underwear and, seen here, Tier 2 pelvic protection. Tier 3 leg protection is worn when the threat is at its highest, such as during route clearance. The small pouches on the 'ladder system' on the front of this man's armour carrier hold 40mm grenades for his rifle's underbarrel launcher. Note the Elcan lightweight day sight, which began to replace the ACOG in 2013. In the left background, the long, wide antennae rising from daysacks indicate men carrying electronic countermeasures equipment. (Crown Copyright 2013)

but retains a standby commitment to support the police under Operation 'Helvetic'; units are now assigned to 38th (Irish) Brigade.

AFGHANISTAN & IRAQ

Immediately after '9/11' the UK began to refocus its military effort on Afghanistan, and then Iraq. In support of US operations in Afghanistan, forces were initially deployed in October 2001 on Operation 'Veritas', the main contribution in ground forces coming from 3rd Cdo Brigade. This 2,000-plus British force was then scaled down to about 300 by mid-2002. From that date NATO's assumption of responsibility for Afghanistan by means of what it called the International Security Assistance Force (ISAF) saw the initiation for the UK of Operation 'Herrick'; British efforts expanded to a strong battalion group, the main part being the Afghanistan Roulement Infantry Battalion (ARIB) responsible for the security of Kabul. First deployment was 2 RGR from Brunei, and this specific commitment continued until April 2008, with nine battalions eventually rotating through the role every six months.

The UK's main effort switched towards an invasion of Iraq in late 2002. UK forces deployed on this Operation 'Telic' in support of a US-led coalition in January 2003, and ground forces attacked into Iraq in March, capturing Basrah the following month. For this initial warfighting phase the UK effort totalled nearly 46,000 personnel, with combat forces based on Headquarters 1st Armd Div with three brigades: 7th Armd, 16th Air Asslt and 3rd

Table 10: Deployments on Operation 'Telic', Iraq

Telic I Jan–July 2003: 1st Armd Div (7th Armd Bde, 16th Air Asslt Bde, 3rd Cdo Bde)

Telic II July–Nov 2003: 3rd Div (19th Mech Bde)

Telic III Nov 2003–Apr 2004: 20th Armd Bde

Telic IV Apr–Nov 2004: 1st Mech Bde

Telic V Nov 2004–Apr 2005: 4th Armd Bde

Telic VI Apr–Oct 2005: 12th Mech Bde

Telic VII Oct 2005–May 2006: 7th Armd Bde

Telic VIII May–Nov 2006: 20th Armd Bde

Telic IX Nov 2006–June 2007: 19th Lt Bde

Telic X June–Dec 2007: 1st Mech Bde

Telic XI Dec 2007–June 2008: 4th Mech Bde

Telic XII June–Dec 2008: 7th Armd Bde

Telic XIII Dec 2008–Apr 2009: 20th Armd Bde

Commando. Headquarters 3rd Div relieved HQ 1st Armd Div in July 2003, and command then passed to the British-led Multi-National Division South-East for the remainder of the campaign. British combat forces were reduced to one reinforced brigade in mid-2003, and this level of force was broadly maintained through a total of 13 rotations (shown in **Table 10**) until the operation ended in April 2009. Once combat operations eased after the capture of Basrah, British troops expected to deal with stabilization operations, but from April 2004 they became sucked into an increasingly intense counter-insurgency operation.

The Foxhound light protected patrol vehicle (LPPV), here mounting two GPMGs, was an 'urgent operational requirement' for Afghanistan. It entered service in 2012, and will be retained for future use by the 'light protected mobility' infantry battalions under Army 2020. Developed from the US General Dynamics Ocelot, the 4x4 Foxhound LPPV carries a crew of two plus four infantrymen.
(Crown Copyright 2012)

Simultaneously with the height of the insurgency in Iraq, the UK greatly expanded its effort in Afghanistan (shortened to 'Afghan' in the Army's current vernacular). From the onset of operations in December 2001 the scale of effort had been based on a divisional headquarters and a multi-national brigade, of which the ARIB was part. The first divisional headquarters was the UK's 3rd Div, handing over subsequently to other NATO countries. From late summer 2003 NATO began to expand outwards from Kabul, eventually covering the whole country by October 2006. Higher command was enlarged to the corps level in May 2006, with HQ ARRC being the first to deploy and being relieved by the US in February 2007 and thereafter.

In July 2006 British ground forces were committed to Helmand Province in the south-west, initially to conduct stabilization and capacity-building but rapidly becoming engulfed in another intense counter-insurgency campaign. Task Force Helmand is based on a reinforced brigade group with considerable

OPERATION 'HERRICK', AFGHANISTAN

These three figures show the latest operational clothing and personal equipment developments, with MTP now universal.

1: Lieutenant, 3rd Battalion Mercian Regiment (Staffords), 2010

This platoon commander has a Mk 7 helmet covered in scrim and with HMNVS mounting plate, PRR and headset, and ESS ballistic eye protection. His under-armour UBACS shirt displays the ISAF patch and his battalion TRF on the right sleeve, and would also have the 7th Armd Bde patch and Afghan flag on the left; above both sleeve pockets are strips of reflective 'Identification Friend or Foe' tape. The Osprey Mk 4 armour is rigged with various MOLLE pouches, and shows a personalized 'zap' patch on the chest. His kit includes an ammunition grab bag on the left hip, a daysack on the back containing the Bowman PRC 354 radio and with a Camelbak water carrier (in Woodland DPM) on the right side. Note Oakley patrol gloves, Garmin Foretrex navigation system on the wrist, and pelvic protection. His L85A2 rifle has a 'picatinny rail' and standard operational modifications.

1a: Mercian Regt TRF on right sleeve pocket.

1b: Left sleeve pocket, with Union flag, Afghan flag and 7th Armd Bde patches. Both sleeve pockets contain tourniquets, and the black item hanging out here is a tourniquet cover.

2: Dog handler, 1st Military Working Dog Regiment, 2013

Working dogs are vital assets in searching for IEDs, weapons and explosives. This female search-dog handler wears the Royal Army Veterinary Corps TRF on her right sleeve pocket with the ISAF patch. She is similarly dressed and equipped to H1, but has HMNVS mounted on her helmet and a medical pouch on the right side of her body armour, and carries the L22A1 carbine.

3: Private, 2nd Battalion Duke of Lancaster's Regiment, 2013

This infantryman is operating a Vallon VMH-3 mine detector. As shown here, the weight of Osprey armour saw soldiers largely dispensing with MOLLE pouches attached to their plate-carriers and instead wearing PLCE under the armour. Ballistic 'eyepro', body armour and pelvic protection had all become mandatory for operations 'outside the wire' – i.e. outside permanent bases. Note the 1st Mech Bde patch on his left sleeve pocket (**3a**), and the 'zap' patch on his daysack. This shows his unit TRF (yellow glider on green ground, outlined maroon, commemorating the antecedent 1st Bn Border Regt's World War II service in 1st Air-Landing Bde of 1st Airborne Div); a Union flag; his 'zap number', allowing identification of casualties without using names; and blood group.

1

1a

1b

2

3

3a

WH1212
LT OPOS

TAZA

1

Table 11: Deployments on Operation 'Herrick', Afghanistan

Herrick I–III 2003–06: reinforced battalion groups (ARIB)	Herrick XII Apr–Oct 2010: 4th Mech Bde
	Herrick XIII Oct 2010–Apr 2011: 16th Air Asslt Bde
Herrick IV May–Nov 2006: 16th Air Asslt Bde	Herrick XIV Apr–Oct 2011: 3rd Cdo Bde
Herrick V Nov 2006–Apr 2007: 3rd Cdo Bde	Herrick XV Oct 2011–Apr 2012: 20th Armd Bde
Herrick VI Apr–Oct 2007: 12th Mech Bde	Herrick XVI Apr–Oct 2012: 12th Mech Bde
Herrick VII Oct 2007–Apr 2008: 52nd Inf Bde	Herrick XVII Oct 2012–Apr 2013: 4th Mech Bde
Herrick VIII Apr–Oct 2008: 16th Air Asslt Bde	Herrick XVIII Apr–Oct 2013: 1st Mech Bde
Herrick IX Oct 2008–Apr 2009: 3rd Cdo Bde	Herrick XIX Oct 2013–June 2014: 7th Armd Bde
Herrick X Apr–Oct 2009: 19th Lt Bde	Herrick XX June–Dec 2014: 20th Armd Bde
Herrick XI Oct 2009–Apr 2010: 11th Lt Bde	

logistic and enabling forces in support. Combat operations continued until June 2013, when Afghan government forces assumed primacy for security. Since 'Herrick IV', 17 rotations (shown in **Table 11**) by ten brigades will have served in Helmand up to the UK's withdrawal at the end of 2014. During particularly tough periods between 2008 and 2010 the brigade was reinforced by the Theatre Reserve Battalion based in Cyprus, the whole force reaching a peak of around 9,000 in late 2009.

UNIFORMS

The authority for all uniforms and dress distinctions is enshrined in Army Dress Regulations, which were last formally updated in 2007. As certain items of dress are in a constant state of change, especially in the case of combat uniforms, regular amendments are made. No deviation from any authorized pattern of clothing is allowed and no new badge is permitted without authority, but the Army has long had a reputation for some lack of uniformity, especially amongst its officers, and while deployed on operations. During such postings the soldiers too have acquired a casual, if pragmatic approach to dress and personal equipment. Apart from practicality, there is a degree of fashion in such choices; clothing and kit that is considered the height of cool is described as 'ally' (though the author has been unable to track down the origin of this adjective).

Unsurprisingly, given its unbroken heritage, the Army's more formal uniforms are governed by largely historical traditions; but given the number of amalgamations and structural changes over the years, dress distinctions can be hard to track. While the wearing today of Full Dress is limited, its details are important, as they govern the various colours and

Full Dress: a drill sergeant from 1st Bn Scots Guards gives orders while dressing the line. Note the regiment's thistle collar badge. The Full Dress tunics of the Foot Guards also have differing button arrangements: Grenadiers – six evenly spaced; Coldstream – six in three pairs; Scots – three sets of three; Irish – two sets of four; Welsh – five evenly spaced. Bearskin plumes also differ, in order: white on left, red on right, none, blue on right, and white/green/white on left. (Crown Copyright 2013)

adornments on modern uniforms. Thus the historical 'facing' colours for regiments and corps are perpetuated today in items such as ceremonial uniforms and mess dress. Likewise, certain accoutrements such as stable belts and shoulder lanyards owe their colours to these historical precedents.

ORDERS OF DRESS

The system governing today's uniforms is largely the result of the changes made in the 1960s following the end of conscription. The universal Battle Dress was replaced with two main types: a parade uniform, based on what had been officers' Service Dress, and a new 'combat' uniform. Aside from Full Dress, or what remained of it, the various uniforms were grouped by 1971 into 14 Orders of Dress, all numbered according to function. The evolution of these groupings has led to a degree of mixing up of the numbers, but the following are extant:

Full Dress (see Plates A & B)

Full Dress is described as 'the ultimate statement of tradition and regimental identity in uniform', and out of it come all of the special details displayed in other orders of dress. While Full Dress is very evident in the Household Division whilst performing ceremonial duties, for the vast bulk of the Army its wear has been in abeyance since the Great War. However, it is retained by drummers, buglers, trumpeters and pipers when they are found on the strength of units, and it was readopted by many bands in the 1990s. The Royal Gibraltar Regiment also wears Full Dress for its regular ceremonial functions.

Its main features are as they were last fully established in 1881. The tunic is limited to three colours: scarlet, dark blue or green. Trousers and tight overalls are in dark blue except for three regiments: RDG and R IRISH wear green, and KRH wear cherry-red. All pre-1881 facing colours were reintroduced in the 1920s and 1930s and are seen on uniforms today. Special headdress is also worn, and all of these, such as the drummers' cloth helmet, are also as ordered in 1881. Scottish regiments have markedly different uniforms, most obviously their tartan kilts and trews and their headdress. While it is not classified as Full Dress, in particular circumstances a blue frock coat is worn by certain officers, usually general officers and bandmasters.

Drum Major O'Connor, 1st Bn Staffordshire Regiment, 2002, in typical line infantry Full Dress with the yellow facings and Stafford Knot badge of this regiment. He wears the infantry 1881 Pattern blue cloth helmet, and drum majors' gold lace on his tunic instead of the crown lace worn by the drummers (see Plate B2) . Note tasselled bugle cords, and drum major's sash. (Staffords Museum)

No. 1 Dress: soldiers from 2nd Bn Princess of Wales's Royal Regt preparing for public duties in London, 2012; this was the last line battalion to undertake this role. They wear 'blues' with the distinctions for a Royal regiment: a red band on the forage cap, and red piping on the shoulder straps. Note the regimental 'Tiger' badge on the left sleeve. (2 PWRR)

Northern Ireland, 2009: 2nd Bn Princess of Wales's Royal Regt was the last operational resident battalion in the Province, and these two soldiers wear typical No. 8 Dress and equipment for that time. The left-hand soldier, in a DPM windproof smock and a Vest, Tactical, Load-Carrying, has a PRR with a hand microphone clipped to its pouch. The khaki beret became universal for all infantry except for RRF following the FIS 2004 changes; the Fusiliers retain dark blue berets with their red-and-white feather hackle. The PWRR's blue and yellow regimental TRF is also worn behind the cap badge. (2 PWRR)

No. 1 & No. 3 Dress – Ceremonial (see Plate A)

No. 1 Dress – Temperate Ceremonial – evolved from the blue patrol jacket of the late 19th century. Worn rarely, after World War II it became a soldiers' parade uniform but was not universally introduced. Today the use of 'blues' is largely restricted to colour parties and bands, but units outside the Household Division undertaking public duties were issued No. 1 Dress to smarten them up. It is also worn by cadets and staff at the Royal Military Academy Sandhurst. The dark blue jacket is worn by all except the SCOTS, who wear Archer Green, the R IRISH in Piper Green, and the RIFLES and Gurkhas in Rifle Green. Regimental distinctions other than authorized badges are limited to shoulder-strap piping in various colours.

Trousers are in the same colour and largely as for Full Dress, with varying widths and colours of sideseam striping according to regiment or corps. The main item of headwear is the peaked 'forage cap', although there are regimental differences: SCOTS wear the Glengarry, R IRISH the Caubeen, Gurkhas the Kilmarnock, and a number – RTR, RRF, RIFLES, PARA and AAC – wear their distinctive berets. No. 3 Dress – Warm Weather Ceremonial – is a white cotton drill version of No. 1 issued to units in hot-weather stations, with trousers and headdress as for No. 1 Dress.

No. 2, No. 4 and No. 6 Dress – Parade Uniform/Service Dress (see Plate B)

No. 2 Dress – Temperate Parade, otherwise known as Service Dress (SD) – evolved from the khaki serge service dress that was introduced in 1902 and was the Army's field uniform until the introduction of Battle Dress in 1938. The latter's demise in the 1960s saw the reintroduction of a khaki SD for all ranks for parades. A number of regimental variations existed until 2009, when Future Army Dress brought in a universal pattern (although different tunics are worn by the Foot Guards and SCOTS). Trousers are in the same colour except for those worn by the RDG, KRH and R IRISH as noted above. Headdress on parade is the same as for No. 1 Dress, except that Gurkhas wear a stiffened slouch hat. A variety of different forms of headdress, such as SD caps and sidehats, are worn off parade.

Introduced as a warm-weather version, No. 4 Dress – Warm Weather Parade – is in a lightweight stone-coloured cloth, but other details are exactly as for No. 2 Dress. The uniform is often worn by officers in temperate climates in the summer (being referred to as 'summer service dress') but should not be worn on parade. No. 6 Dress – Warm Weather Parade Uniform – is a bush jacket worn as the other ranks' version of No. 4 Dress, but the jacket is cut very differently, with an open neck and short sleeves. All distinctions are as for SD.

No. 10 and No. 11 Dress – Mess Dress (see Plate C)

Temperate Mess Dress for officers, warrant officers and senior NCOs is the oldest form of dress, having evolved from mid-19th century undress shell and stable jackets. Colours and distinctions on jackets generally follow Full Dress conventions, although jackets and waistcoats often bear elaborate lace and piping. Two versions are worn: 1902 Pattern, with a high collar and full-length waistcoat; and 1936 Pattern, with a lapelled front, white shirt, bow-tie, and low-cut waistcoat. Trousers, and overalls for officers, are as for No. 1 Dress ceremonial. No. 11 Dress – the warm-weather version of Mess Dress – is in white cotton and comes in both patterns, with regimental cummerbunds worn at the waist in place of waistcoats.

No. 7, No. 13 and No. 14 Dress – Barrack Dress (see Plate C)

Barrack Dress derived from fatigue uniform and was introduced as a daily in-barracks working dress. In its issued form it comprised a khaki shirt and green pullover – the Army's ubiquitous Jersey, Heavy Wool or 'woolly-pully', which was also part of Combat Dress – with green barrack-dress or khaki denim trousers. For many years seen as a uniform for 'office wallahs', and worn less and less, barrack dress began to be reissued from 2009 with the direction that it was to be worn more often.

Officers and warrant officers invariably wear a smarter version with coloured regimental pullovers, various officers' pattern shirts and ties, and SD or other trousers. A colourful effect is enhanced by canvas stable belts, every regiment and corps sporting its own colours and variety of pattern. Worn with a pullover, this is No. 13 Dress; in shirtsleeve order it is No. 14 Dress. There is also a warm-weather version – No. 7 Dress – made in a light fabric of a similar stone colour to No. 4 Dress. Headdress in all cases is the same as for SD off parade.

No. 12 Dress – Protective Clothing

Another descendant of fatigue uniform, No. 12 Dress is limited to two items – denim coveralls, and the working clothing for Army chefs. Coveralls are held by all units for dirty jobs but are generally issued to mechanics and those working with armour. They are universally green except for the RTR, who have black.

No. 5, No. 8 and No. 9 Dress – Combat Dress (see Plates D to H)

Combat Dress is worn today in preference to all other forms; it is the uniform in which soldiers wish to be seen, and the image the public now most associates with the fighting man. Many parades, especially following a return from operational tours, now see soldiers marching in Combat Dress. It is comfortable, and – while there is a natural tendency for NCOs to attempt to smarten up the soldier even when he is wearing Combats – it is eminently practical.

Nevertheless, combat clothing and personal equipment are often the least 'uniform' of items, since many soldiers buy their own, available commercially, to overcome perceived (often wrongly so) failings in issued items. Harsh operational conditions lead to every

Jordan, 2006: company command group from 2nd Bn Royal Regt of Fusiliers during Exercise 'Saffron Sands'. Stationed in Cyprus, 2 RRF was then the Theatre Reserve Battalion for possible reinforcement of operations in Iraq or Afghanistan. These soldiers wear No. 5 Dress Desert DPM with Enhanced Combat Body Armour; the officer on the left has acquired his own knee pads, gloves and thigh pack. The battalion TRF is in regimental style: 'SECOND/ FUSILIERS' in black, on a black-edged drab patch matching the clothing. Note also the red/ yellow regimental helmet patch. (RHQ RRF)

A soldier from 3rd Bn Mercian Regt poses to give a good view of the profile of the Mk 7 helmet. The ESS ballistic eye protection ('eyepro') has interchangeable lenses in clear, yellow and dark hardened plastic. The MTP-camouflage UBACS has padded forearms; his TRF and ISAF patch are as shown on Plate H1. (RHQ Mercian)

possible variation of dress and equipment (as the accompanying photographs and plates testify), and the application of a variety of standards of appearance. Beards were often permitted in some locations in Afghanistan, although Queen's Regulations demand that only a moustache may be worn, beards being permitted normally only for assault pioneer sergeants in infantry units.

Combat Dress has evolved constantly since its first introduction in the 1960s. By the 1990s, two versions were on issue: No. 8 Dress, for wear in temperate conditions, and No. 9 for tropical conditions. Both were made in 'Woodland' DPM, the tropical version being in much lighter material. A Desert DPM version had been issued for Operation 'Granby' and subsequent desert campaigns, and this became No. 5 Dress.

Combats received a major makeover during the 1990s with the Combat Soldier 95 programme. The original DPM camouflage was retained, but the modern design, fabrics and layered system of 'Combats 95' were a major improvement on the original. While the Jersey, Heavy Wool was also retained, the green combat shirt (which replaced the hated Shirt, Khaki Flannel in the late 1980s) was discarded for a DPM shirt, and there were additional items of layering for cold and hot weather. Rank badges, long largely hidden under load-carrying equipment, moved to a buttoned strap on the centre of the chest. Particular relief from wet weather was provided by Gore-Tex DPM waterproofs, which saw the end of the less-than-waterproof green poncho.

In the 21st century, personal clothing and equipment began to be examined holistically under the Future Integrated Soldier Technology (FIST) programme. The extreme demands of operations saw many FIST developments brought into service early, and FIST was superseded by PECOC: Personal Equipment and Common Operational Clothing. This led to the Personal Clothing System (PCS), which replaced all DPM items – temperate, tropical and desert – with an entirely new universal design in Multi-Terrain Pattern (MTP) from March 2010, with issues completed across the Army by mid-2013. Called PCS

Typically heavily-laden soldiers from 1st Bn Duke of Lancaster's Regt negotiating Afghan terrain during 'Herrick XVI', 12th Mech Bde's tour in 2012. The 'jimpy' gunner has the half-collar fitted to his Osprey vest, and by this time helmet 'scrim' was a standard feature for most infantrymen.
(Crown Copyright 2012)

(Combat Uniform), it was initially based on the Combat 95 design. It continues to evolve, with cold-weather and hot-weather versions, including the Under Body Armour Combat Shirt (UBACS) originally issued in Desert DPM, which has camouflage-fabric arms but a plain, lighter, ventilated torso. Originally all 'shirts' were ordered to be worn with sleeves rolled down and the shirt untucked at the waist ('down and out'), but from 2013 a new lightweight shirt can be worn 'up and in'.

Boots were not included in PECOC but were subject to separate study. Ankle boots and cloth puttees had given way to far superior Boots, Combat, High in the mid-1980s, and to later models including desert boots. Of all clothing items, boots have received the most criticism over the years; many soldiers have bought their own for wear in the field, and the Army has procured commercially available boots such as Lowa and Meindl for recent operational use. A new footwear system from 2013 provides an all-brown range of five varieties of boot, each variety having two models.

Chemical, biological, radiological and nuclear (CBRN) suits continue to be issued in Woodland and Desert DPM. The greyish-coloured papers on his arms, leg and boot are for detecting chemical agents. This soldier also wears the latest General Service Respirator, which has replaced the SR10. (Crown Copyright 2012)

Personal equipment

Deciding what the footsoldier carries is a constant balancing act between requirements and weight. The introduction of nylon Personal Load-Carrying Equipment (PLCE) in the 1980s to replace 58 Pattern webbing improved the situation markedly, especially with bergan rucksacks and daysacks replacing the inadequate 58 Pattern Large Pack, and a new entrenching tool largely

The infantry's core role: dismounted close combat. Here a soldier from 3 PARA fights through an Afghan compound during 'Herrick VIII'. With his Osprey armour he wears typical PLCE and a daysack in Woodland DPM, with a Bowman PRC 354 radio on his right hip. (Crown Copyright 2008)

Osprey Mk 4 armour, showing light and complete fighting order. Osprey Mk 1, introduced in late 2006, and Mk 2, had large external ballistic plates; Mk 3 was the first with internal plates. The Mk 4 armour is the same as Mk 3 but in an MTP cover, and Mk 4A, introduced in mid-2013, provides improved hip plates and a patrol collar. The Pouch Attachment Ladder System (PALS) provides fixing points for MOLLE. (Illustration courtesy CQC Ltd)

Light Fighting Order

Non Slip Shoulders

NB: When no collar is fitted to the vest, the collar tabs are tucked under the main vest shoulder join.

Grab Handles

OPS Panel with adjustable T Bar fittings

T Bar Adjustment

Complete Fighting Order

Showing Full Collar. Brassards. Cummerbunds & Shoulder Guards

Full Collar

Shoulder Guards

Brassards

Brassards

The OPS Panel is removed. Replaced with Cummerbunds fitted with adjustable front webbing straps

Half Collar

doing away with cumbersome lightweight picks and shovels. Personal modifications to PLCE were possible by buying commercially available kit, but PLCE itself stayed largely unchanged from its original design except for pouch fastenings and the adoption of DPM instead of olive green; all items are now being made in MTP. (To a soldier, his harness is still 'webbing'.) Armoured infantry found PLCE cumbersome, and many purchased chest harnesses and tactical vests; this prompted the Army to procure quantities of both in Woodland and Desert DPM for general operational issue.

However, PECOC has led to radical changes in load-carrying due to the integration of body armour. Troops in Northern Ireland were long accustomed to wearing 'flak jackets', and the 1980s saw the introduction of INIBA – Individual Northern Ireland Body Armour – worn under the combat jacket. Outside the Province body armour was not available until Combat Body

Armour (CBA), worn outside clothing, was provided for Operation 'Granby'. By the onset of Operation 'Telic', Enhanced CBA, with a ballistic plate on the chest, had appeared. The scale and intensity of enemy attacks in Iraq and Afghanistan led to Kestrel armour being provided for vulnerable vehicle crews from late 2005 while Osprey armour was being developed.

Osprey, introduced from late 2006 and by 2013 in a Mk 4A version, undoubtedly provides excellent protection, but at the inevitable expense of mobility, especially when combined with the new three-tier pelvic protection system. Osprey was also intended to provide a carrier for much personal equipment by way of the attached Modular Lightweight Load-carrying Equipment (MOLLE, pronounced 'Molly'); but the weight of the MOLLE pouches combined with that of the armour has proved unpopular, and has seen the return of PLCE on lighter yokes for wear under the armour. The soldier's habit of placing items such as pistols, bayonets and other clutter on the chest of the Osprey plate-carrier was forbidden from 2011, due to the additional facial injuries that these items could cause in an explosion.

The 1980s had also seen the demise of the Mk 3 steel helmet and the introduction in 1986 of the Mk 6 made from composite materials. In 2005 the Mk 6A helmet replaced the Mk 6, until the Mk 7 was brought into service from June 2009. This, with ballistic eye protection ('eyepro'), Osprey and pelvic protection, are compulsory wear for all high-threat environments.

South of Basrah, Iraq, April 2003: the mortar platoon of 1st Bn Royal Regiment of Fusiliers in action during 'Telic I'. As an armoured infantry battalion, 1 RRF carried its eight 81mm mortars mounted in FV432 Mk 2 tracked armoured vehicles. Note the mixed items of Woodland and Desert DPM then worn. The Fusilier at left shows the regimental red/yellow helmet patch, and on his right sleeve the 'FIRST/FUSILIERS' TRF above the patch of 7th Armd Bde – the only formation to wear its badge on the right arm. (Crown Copyright 2003)

Badges on Combat Dress

For the sake of operational security, regimental and corps dress distinctions were once largely forbidden on Combat Dress, although regimental berets and cap badges were a common feature in the field. Formation badges were rarely seen on uniforms; but the ending of the Cold War and the coincidental onset of the First Gulf War saw an almost immediate proliferation of these patches on the sleeves of combat jackets. They were quickly followed by the introduction of Tactical Recognition Flashes (TRFs) for more or less every unit in the Army. These are the successors to the 'battle patches' of the World Wars, and also take the form of a cloth patch worn on the upper sleeve, though now attached with Velcro rather than sewn on.

In 2003 the Army officially standardized the design and wearing of all cloth patches, although unit variations remain common, and a rash of unauthorized badges tends to break out during active operations. Unit TRFs are now worn on the upper right sleeve, with formation patches worn on the upper left. At the same time a small Union flag has become universally worn, placed on the left sleeve above formation patches.

Typical example of the medals awarded in the last 25 years. Colonel Simon Banton wears No.2 Dress with the red 'tabs' indicating General Staff service, but still sports the Mercian Regt's cerise, green and buff lanyard – on his right shoulder, rather than the left for other ranks as in Plate B1.

He displays, from left to right: Order of the British Empire; Gulf War Medal with clasp '16 Jan–28 Feb 1991'; General Service Medal with clasp 'Northern Ireland'; NATO Medal for Former Yugoslavia with clasp; NATO Medal for Kosovo with clasp ('2' indicating two tours, and silver oak-leaf denoting Queen's Commendation for Valuable Service); Iraq Medal; Operational Service Medal with clasp 'Afghanistan'; Queen's Golden Jubilee Medal; Queen's Diamond Jubilee Medal; Accumulated Campaign Service Medal; and US Bronze Star. (Author's photo)

Medals

One major difference readily apparent when comparing photographs of soldiers on parade 20 years ago and today is the sheer number of campaign medals on their chests. Historically, the British Army has awarded medals only sparingly when compared with other armies, and almost exclusively for active operations.

Until 1990 it was common to see just a single medal – the General Service Medal 1962–2007 with the clasp 'Northern Ireland'; some soldiers would have the UN medal issued for Cyprus, and rather fewer the South Atlantic Medal 1982 for the Falklands conflict. However, the 1990s saw the proliferation of various UN and NATO medals for service in the Balkans (though many soldiers regard these in a different light from British medals).

In 1992 the Gulf War Medal was issued for service in that theatre in 1990–91; clasps '2 Aug 1990' and '16 Jan–28 Feb 1991' mark, respectively, those who were serving with the Kuwait Liaison Team at the date of the Iraqi invasion, and service in the war-fighting phase of the liberation.

In 1994 the Accumulated Campaign Service Medal was instituted to mark 36 months of aggregated British operational service since 1969 (i.e. service under NATO, UN or EU commands does not count towards eligibility).

Since 2000, two further British campaign medals have been awarded. The first is the Operational Service Medal (OSM) 2000, which replaces the GSM except for Northern Ireland service. The medal has so far been issued with three different ribbons and clasps, for service in Sierra Leone, Democratic Republic of Congo[1] and Afghanistan. The second is the Iraq Medal 2003, for Operation 'Telic' between 2003 and 2009; a clasp '19 Mar–28 Apr 2003' was issued for the invasion phase.

---

1 For Operation 'Coral', 14 June–10 September 2003, when modest numbers of specialist personnel took part in the French-led EU 'Artemis' mission to Bunia, Ituri Province. This was to support inadequate UN security efforts during an episode of the endemic tribal warfare in the eastern Congo.

Gallantry decorations

In 1993–94 major changes were made to the system for the award of gallantry medals, orders and decorations, largely doing away with the distinctions historically made between awards for officers and other ranks. Awards of the Distinguished Conduct Medal (DCM), Military Medal (MM) and the British Empire Medal (BEM), once very proudly seen as the 'soldiers' medals', were discontinued, with soldiers and NCOs henceforth eligible to receive the Military Cross (MC) and to be made a Member of the Order of the British Empire (MBE). A new award for gallantry – the Conspicuous Gallantry Cross (CGC) – was introduced, ranking immediately below the Victoria Cross and above the Military Cross; and the Queen's Commendation for Valuable Service now supplements the Mention in Dispatches.

Since 2000 there have been three awards of the Victoria Cross made to British soldiers, one for Iraq and two (posthumously) for Afghanistan.

FURTHER READING

There are numerous printed sources covering recent campaigns, but surprisingly little on modern British Army structures and organizational details. Charles Heyman's *The British Army Guide 2012–2013* (Barnsley, 2011), published originally from 1984 as pocket guides, is invaluable. On badges, see Robin Hodges, *British Army Badges* (Devizes, 2005); while now outdated by all post-2005 changes, this is a superb reference work of continued relevance. Most badge changes and the plethora of TRFs can be found in *Badge Notes* by Gary Gibbs in each quarterly issue of *The Bulletin of the Military Historical Society*.

Official open sources are available online. See especially www.army.mod.uk, although many pages are not always up to date. An annual brochure is made available on www.army.newsdeskmedia.com, the latest being *The British Army 2012*. Follow links for updates on Army 2020 and the Reserves. The MoD's www.defenceimagery.mod.uk has some excellent photographs, many of them downloadable, although major restrictions are imposed on reuse. Any number of unofficial websites exist, but a good source for details on dress and equipment and comprehensive pictures can be found at www.militaryphotos.net by following links to the British Army.

INDEX